Cooking with Hot Peppers—Plus Other Delicious and Mouth-Watering Recipes

Peter Ewanchuk

VANTAGE PRESS
New York

Parents should bear in mind that hot peppers should be kept out of the reach of children.

Recipes herein have not been tested by the publisher.

CONTENTS

ACKNOWLEDGEMENT

I would like to give credit and thanks to those people who cultivated this land for a better life for everyone, especially those in North America, and made farm products possible. I would also like to thank those who originated the homemade foods which are used in this book. Now I can repay them by preserving their recipes in this volume.

PREFACE

The recipes in this cookbook are selected to become the most preferred and used in your life. They are designed with a contents and general headings that will make it easy to find the recipe you want. It is a small book, but with many recipes. You will probably look at these recipes with many preferences in mind. As many recipes are included, it will take a long time to try them all. Although this book contains more than the making of one, it is not too big to handle. It has many outstanding recipes. It contains the best and most common homecooked foods. Its price is reasonable so that any home can afford one. It gives you the recipes and tells you how to prepare food with easy to follow instructions so that you can have more flavor and nutrition in your food. By using these recipes more, not only will you enjoy better food, you will cut your food bills considerably, just as they were done by people long ago, helping them to live economically by preparing their own food. These recipes are written for the benefit of those who want them. It is a gift to be a good cook of your favorite foods. You can be too if you follow the instructions in this book.

If you want to live more economically, it is suggested this is the book for you! Enjoy your homemade food!

PREFACE OF A BOOK COVER DESIGN

This book cover design is very appropriate to the recipes in this cookbook. Since these homemade foods originated in the country, it makes sense to have a country scene on the book cover, where all the produce is raised. Cereal crops are sown and harvested for food, as well as feed for livestock and poultry. Dairy products come from the country as well. Vegetables and fruits are also planted. So many things can be raised and planted on a farm. Wild berries and cherries grow on their own, which is excellent for fruit. The farmer feeds everyone, both in the country and in the cities. He feeds everything as well, including animals, birds, and insects. The farm is like a mother to everyone. She provides for and feeds her children. She is a generous and prosperous mother, both at the table and on the farm. Produce does not come from the store or from the table: it comes from the farm.

Everyone depends on farms for produce. If there was no farm, there would be famine in the land, and the rest of the world would feel the effect. Farming came to be the first thing in cultivation for life and profit; that was how our ancestors lived economically. Homemade food was originated here before the country was developed. Since it was created on the farm, the cover's country scene will resonate throughout the cookbook in each recipe. Homemade food is the oldest kind of nourishment and remains the best and the most economical. Indeed, it sounds new and appealing all over again.

Although more recipes were created and perfected from homemade foods, the constant creation of more recipes continued to a point where foods were poorly prepared. Careless preparation can make food taste different, often lacking flavor. Two different cooks may be preparing the same kind of food, using the same ingredients. However, there is often a big difference in how the two cooks prepare it. One may use more of the same ingredients than the other, or one may be timing ingredients while the other does not. Herein lies the difference: one will have more flavor, the other less.

People have abused food and learned to make junk food . . . there was a time when junk food had never been heard of. Fast foods also came to the fore. They weren't better foods; they were only more expensive, reminding people that homemade food was better. With the younger generation, homemade foods have been forgotten, for the most part.

Hopefully, the recipes in this cookbook will help remind them of how good homemade food is.

Homemade food has more natural flavor, more nutrition, and is fairly frugal. It is about 99 percent free from chemicals. During the Great Depression (and even today), if there are many children in the family to feed and the parents do not have a decent job, homemade foods are helpful. If they know how to feed them economically, it can help them save a lot of money. To buy ingredients at the store and prepare your own food at home is economically sound. On the farm, however, you have your own food and it is fresh. Preparing food at home is even more economical. Under certain conditions, the food is even better.

On the cover of this book, there is an illustration of the country. Though the picture says a lot, the following story will tell you even more.

For the farmers to have land for grain crops, they had to clear the bush that had the richest black soil. It was only in the bush that the soil was at its best. To have so much land, they even created deforestation, not leaving any trees or shrubs in the way and leaving the land open and flat. So the bush grew on the rich, black soil, and it was very favorable for farming and vegetables.

In the early days, they didn't need education to cultivate the land or to do other hard work to open the land. They were only fortunate if they were big and strong, So that with the sweat of their brow they could eat bread.

They yearned for bare land—they considered the bush useless—and they looked at the country fields as being more useful and productive. Canada is one of the biggest breadbaskets in the world! They have more grain than they need for themselves. The province of Manitoba has one of the richest soils in Canada. The chief industry in Canada is farming. If an artist wanted to paint a farm scene, he wouldn't find much composition on a farmer's field. If he added a few trees or shrubs to create composition, though, he's not capturing the farmer's idea and purpose. Although some farm scenes have more composition than others, the best thing an artist can do is include some birds and tall grass in the open areas. An artist's conception may do well for an illustration, but it won't help suggest its realism. A photographer doesn't always look for composition; yet, his photos are still accepted.

The bush will grow only on black soil, which is the best for farming. The farmers were more conscious of the land where the bush grew, than they were conscious of the black soil in the bush that was so beneficial for farming. They had to shed the bush to be able to sow and harvest grain.

ABOUT THE AUTHOR

The reader might be wondering who is the cook who wrote these recipes? How and where did the recipes originate? Now, think of where the food products grow, where the people first began their lives, where they prepared their first homemade food. We can now say that settlement and life began in the country, the motherland, which they were able to depend on. I learned from those people how to prepare these recipes and soon they became my favorite foods. In those days, fast foods were unheard of. So wherever I moved, I remembered and used the recipes. They had been my favorite foods, I had never thought about writing recipes for a cookbook. I had no doubt that it might possibly be one of the best selling books in the country.

With time, I became more creative. I perfected this food and even created some new recipes. For instance, I started cooking with hot peppers and using garlic extensively for both flavor and good health. Since I began using hot peppers in my foods, my health improved. It is a known fact that hot peppers and garlic are good for your health and for minor cures. For those who cannot use these ingredients, you have the option to omit them and/or use less salt. If the cook does not have some ingredients stated in the recipes that are less important, he/she can still do well without one or two ingredients.

These recipes are the oldest and are here to stay. Like all good material, they never wear out.

The recipes in this cookbook are my favorites. Most of the recipes are for selected, most-preferred foods, and commonly used foods in everyday life. They are healthy and nutritious, as homemade foods usually are.

According to my recipes and the experience I have had, I am one of the best cooks in North America. But anyone who follows my recipes carefully can equal me as a good cook. But I am not the best cook to try the recipes of other authors. I still can learn something from other cooks. I have never worked as a cook; I've only cooked for myself at home. Not only do I explain the recipes in this cookbook; I try to tell readers how to prepare the food so it will retain flavor and nutrition. To do this, you have to time your ingredients. Remember, preparation is very important! Take a look at two cooks, for example: both cooks can use the same ingredients to prepare the same kind of food, but they will prepare it a little differently. As you look into the recipes in this cookbook, you will find how to prepare. You don't need to be a good cook, but if you follow the instructions in this book, you cannot help preparing your food right.

This is a book that every home should have, even though they might already have many cookbooks. It is not too big and the recipes will serve you well for a long time. For the reasonable price you'll pay for this book, it will help you cut your food bills considerably! You owe it to yourself! Enjoy your life by preparing your own food! Thank you!

—Peter Ewanchuk

ONE

SOUPS

Beef and Vegetable

1 lb. beef, short ribs, or shank	= 454 g.
1 soup bone	= 1
2 small carrots	= 2
1 celery stick	= 1
1 large potato	= 1
1 large onion	= 1
1 cup raw cabbage	= 250 ml
2 tbsps. soup mix	= 25 ml
1 inch long hot pepper	= 1
2 in. piece parsnip	= 15 ml
1 tbsp. salt and 1 tsp. pepper	= 15 ml
3qts. cold water	= 96 ozs.

Pour 3 quarts of water into a gallon pot and let it heat on high temperature. Put the soup bone in first, and let it boil for half hour. You can turn the heat on the 3 o'clock position and put in the meat, carrots, and soup mix. After an hour's boiling, put in the potato (cut up into 1½-in. size). Add whole onion. Add hot pepper and salt and pepper. Cut up celery into ¼-inch pieces and cut up the cabbage and put these in the final 30–40 minutes. Good taste depends largely on the meat; if you get a soup bone with gummy meat, it is the best! Hot pepper can go in the same time as potatoes. To obtain good flavor in the soup, it is well to use half the amount of salt and pepper at the beginning and the other half in the last half hour. The first half will get in the ingredients while they are cooking, and the rest of the salt will retain the flavor. If it's all put in at the beginning, it will boil out and lose some flavor. Good water helps to make better soup. Will serve 7 or more.

- Humans have more variety in food and preparing it than any other living creatures.
- Every worker enjoys the labor of his own hand, and so every cook enjoys the food of his or her own hand.
- Where is salt most noticed? In food that doesn't need any.

Pea Soup

½ lb. meat	=	227 g.
½ cup peas	=	125 ml
1½ qts. water	=	54 ozs.
½ tsp. salt and ½ tsp. black pepper	=	2 ml
1 onion	=	1
1 small carrot	=	1
1 potato	=	1
½-in. long piece of hot pepper	=	½

First, soak hard peas in water for 6 hours. Pour 1½ quarts of water into a large pot and let it boil at high heat. Put meat, carrot and peas in at the same time. After an hour's boiling, put in the whole onion and cut-up potato. Add salt and pepper and hot pepper. Boil soup for 2¼ hours at 3 o'clock position. If the water dries up, keep adding more water and finish the soup with the same amount of water you added before, 1½ quarts. Yields 6 bowls. Serves 6.

Moose Soup

½ lb. moose meat	=	227g.
1 potato	=	1
1 onion	=	1
2 tbsps. pot barley	=	25 ml
½ tsp. salt and ½ tsp. black pepper	=	2 ml
1½ qts. water	=	54 ozs.
1 in. long parsnip	=	1"
1 in. long hot pepper	=	1"

Heat the water in the pot to a boil. Next, put meat and barley in first. After 1 hour's boiling, add 1 onion and a potato (cut up). Add parsnip, salt and peppers, and boil. Serves 6.

• Parsnip can be added in last ½ hour.
• Salt in soup is needed more than sugar in a cake.
• No recipe writer is an expert. They don't have the expertise to tell the exact amount of ingredients. But an approximation of it still works well!
• A pot holds the most stew.

Smoked Fish Soup

1½ lbs. smoked fish	=	750 g.
1 potato	=	1
1 onion	=	1
1 tbsp. rice or pot barley	=	15 ml
1–2 tbsps. of oil		
2 qts. water	=	64 ozs.
3/4 tbsp. salt and ½ tsp. of pepper	=	10 ml, 3 ml

First, heat the water to a boil. Add rice or pot barley. Let it boil 1 hour before you put in a whole onion and cut-up potato. Add salt and pepper and hot pepper. Let boil at 3 o'clock position for 2 to 2¼ hours. Smoked fish can be added in the last 20 or 25 minutes. Fish fins and tail can be added to soup in the last 30 mins. and boiled.

Beef & Vegetable Soup (Salmon)

½ lb. beef short ribs or shank	= 250 g.
1 large carrot	= 1
1 potato	= 1
1 onion	= 1
2 tbsp. soup mix	= 25 ml
¼ tbsp. salt and ½ tsp. pepper	= 8 ml, 3 ml
1½ qts. water	= 54 ozs.

Meat, carrot and soup mix can be put in first into the boiling water. Put in potato and onion 1 hour later. Add salt and pepper. Hot pepper can be added if preferred. Allow it to boil at 3 o'clock position for 2¼ hours. Smoked fish can be added to the soup in the last 20 mins. One tbsp. of canned salmon can be added to a bowl of hot soup instead. Do not boil it! Yields 6 bowls. Serves 6.

• Soups and cakes have the most ingredients.

• Chopped garlic mixed with butter may get bacteria if it stays for long, not refrigerated properly.

Beef Stew

1 lb. stewing beef	= 454 g.
1 potato	= 1
1 onion	= 1
1 inch long hot pepper	= 1
1 tbsp. salt and ½ tsp. pepper	= 15 ml, 3 ml
2 qts. water	= 64 ozs.

Put stewing beef into boiling water. After 1 hour's boiling, add potato, onion and hot pepper, salt and pepper. Since stewing beef is usually hard and dry meat, it is better to let it boil till it is soft. Not too much water is needed for this kind of stew. This is the stew you can make with least ingredients that can make the soup rich in flavor. Too many ingredients absorb or kill the rich flavor. Stewing beef is the kind of meat that releases the flavor into the soup, so much that it leaves the meat dry and tasteless. So stewing beef is the only kind of meat needing less ingredients for more flavor. Yields 6 bowls. Serves 6.

Cabbage Soup

1 lb. beef shank or short ribs	=	454 g.
3 qts. water	=	96 ozs.
1 potato	=	1
1 carrot	=	1
1 onion	=	1
1 inch long hot peppers	=	1
3 cups cut cabbage	=	3
1 tbsp. salt	=	15 ml
1 tsp. pepper	=	5 ml
2 tbsps. soup mix	=	25 ml

Pour 3 quarts of water into a gallon pot and let boil. Next, put in the meat into the boiling water. Let boil for an hour. Next, put in potato, carrot, onion and hot pepper if preferred. Add salt and pepper. Soup mix can go in with the first ingredients. Let it boil for 2½ hours. For better flavor, have about 2 to 2½ quarts of water left in the pot. Yields 6 bowls. Serves 6.

• Soup boils faster in a small pot than in a big pot with so many things in it.

Enriched Soup

If you want any of your soups made richer by adding just a few more ingredients, try adding a few ingredients to 2½ cups of already prepared soup. These are as follows: Add 1 tablespoon of finely chopped onions; add 1 tablespoon of finely chopped garlic. Let it boil for 5 minutes, then add 1 teaspoon of shredded cheddar cheese to hot soup and stir till it dissolves. Yields 2 bowls. Serves 2.

2 more ingredients can be added to your already made soup as follows: add 2 tablespoons of chopped onions, 1½ tablespoons of coarse cut garlic (3 cloves will do). Cloves can be cut into 2 pieces. Add this to a small amount of water and let it boil for about 10 minutes. The reason a small amount of water is used is so that the soup does not become too thin. The onions have to be well done for better flavor. Another method: onions can be chopped up into bigger pieces and garlic in whole cloves. (More can be added if preferred.) This helps to retain real flavor in the soup. Next, add 2 bowls of soup to a small pot and bring to a boil. The reason for preparing only a small amount for one or two people is because it is a bit too strong for some stomachs. But it acts like a minor cure for stomach disorders.

Chicken Soup

1 chicken	=	1
3 qts. water	=	96 ozs.
2 small carrots	=	2
1 potato	=	1
1 onion	=	1
1 celery stick	=	1
2 tbsps. soup mix or rice	=	25 ml
1 piece hot pepper	=	1
1 piece parsnip	=	1
1 tbsp. salt and 1 tsp pepper	=	15 ml, 5 ml
3/4 cup spaghetti	=	180 ml
¼ cup young dill leaves	=	60 ml

Pour 3 quarts of water into a gallon-size pot and let boil. Put chicken in (cut up in a few pieces). Add carrots, potato, onions and piece of hot pepper, salt and pepper together. In the last half hour put in spaghetti and cut up celery into ¼ inch pieces and put them back in and let boil. Carrots can be taken out after they are half ready and the skin scraped with a spoon, and sliced thin and put back into the pot. Dill leaves can be added in the last 5 minutes. Be sure to keep the same amount of water in the soup as you added at first. Toward the end, taste the soup to see if it's salty enough. If not, add some. Yields 7 bowls. Serves 7.

• Do not have peas and cabbage in the same soup, for they form gas.

Borscht (Beet) Soup

2 heads medium-sized beets	= 2
1 lb. pork neck bones	= 434 g.
1 cup cabbage	= 250 ml
1 large potato	= 1
2 small carrots	= 2
1 onion	= 1
2 tbsps. soup mix	= 25 ml
1 tsp. soft corn off the cob	= 5 ml
1 in. long hot pepper	= 1
1 tbsp. lima beans	= 15 ml
1 celery stick	= 1
2 tbsps. beans	= 25 ml
1 tbsp. salt and 1 tsp. of pepper	= 15 ml, 5 ml
3 qts. water	= 96 ml
2 or 3 tbsps. vinegar	= 50 ml
2 tbsps. flour	= 50 ml
3 tbsps. cereal cream	= 75 ml

Fill a large pot with 3 quarts of water and let boil. Slice the raw beets fine and cut them into strips ¼ inch wide. This is the first ingredient that goes in first, because it takes it long to boil it. Add bones, beans, corn, soup mix and carrots. Boil at 3 o'clock position for 1 hour. Add hot pepper, salt and pepper, potato (cut up), onion and lima beans. Boil carrots and onion whole. When carrots are about half done, take them out and scrape the skin off, then slice them up. Then put them back to boil. Vinegar can be added. Shredded cabbage and sliced celery can be added in the last half hour or 40 minutes. In the last 5 minutes prepare batter by adding about 3 tablespoons cereal cream and flour and liquid from soup from the pot and make batter with a fork. Now put it into the pot and let it boil for 5 minutes. While it's boiling, you can taste the soup to see if it is salty enough. If not, then add more. Yields 7 bowls. Serves 7.

P.S. Just to make a few important comments, this soup can be made with less meat than for other soups. Neck bones are sufficient.

• The most important ingredients to make soup are: meat with a bone, potatoes and onions, salt and pepper and water. These ingredients can still make good soup without adding the lesser ingredients. With 1 or

2 less important ingredients omitted, you won't notice as much difference as in omitting the more important.

TWO

MEALS

Head Cheese

2 pigs' feet	=	1
2 pork hocks	=	1
1 onion	=	1
3/4 head garlic	=	3/4
½ inch long hot pepper	=	h.p.
1 tsp. salt and 1 tsp. pepper	=	3 ml, 3 ml
3 qts. water	=	64 ozs.

Fill a large pot with 3 quarts of water and bring it to a boil. Put all the meat in and let boil at high heat for the first 10 minutes. Then turn the heat down to medium and let boil slowly for 3 hours or more. An onion can be added to it after an hour's boiling. Add the salt and pepper and hot pepper. Garlic can be put in the last half hour. Cut the garlic cloves into two pieces. As it boils, the water usually goes dry. Keep filling in with water, but watch toward the end, that is, to leave 1½ inches of water. If there is too much water, the jelly will be too soft and won't hold together when it will be handled with utensils. And if not enough water, it will be too thick. In some cases, thick jelly is preferred. After you notice the meat is soft and easily comes off the bones, remove it off the heat and let it cool so there won't be too much steam to work. Take the meat out, put it on the plate, and cut it up into small pieces, separating the meat from the bones. Then put the meat back into the pot, spreading it around. One thing we must remember is when boiling, keep the pot partially covered with the lid! To cool it off, the best place to put the pot is in a cold room with the lid off and allow it to breathe as it cools. A cold porch is a good place to keep the meat, but see that it doesn't freeze. It takes a while for it to jell and be ready to eat. Slice it with a knife. Use a large spoon to scoop it out. So delicious with bread. Some eat it with potatoes, but it is better with bread. The second best place to let it jell is in the fridge, but first, allow it to cool off considerably, then put it in the fridge. Always keep it refrigerated. Serves 6.

• In my experience, human beings are the only creatures that prepare food properly and carefully. They are the only creatures who are conscious of the taste in food, whether it is pleasing to the taste or not. It is not in my experience, humans are that way in general.

Chili Sauce

½ lb. ground beef	=	½
2 tbsps. soaked beans	=	25 ml
1 small onion	=	1
1 small piece hot pepper	=	1
4 cloves garlic	=	4
½ tsp. salt and ¼ tsp. pepper	=	2 ml, 1ml
2 tbsps. chili powder	=	25 ml
1 qt. water	=	32 ozs.
2 tbsps. canned tomatoes	=	25 ml
1 tbsp. flour	=	15 ml

Pour 1 quart of water into a pot, bring it to a boil. Then add soaked beans. Let them boil for an hour. Now add ground beef, onion, and hot pepper. Add salt and pepper and hot pepper. Let it boil at 3 o'clock position for a while, then reduce the heat to 300° F = 150° C. Should be ready in 2 hours. Garlic can be added in the last half hour. Chili powder can be added in the last 10 minutes. Taste the sauce to see if it needs anything. Have less water at the end than you had poured—it's supposed to be thick. Two tablespoons of canned tomatoes can be added in the last 5 or 10 minutes. Use 1 tablespoon of juice and make batter with a fork. Let it cool. Serves 5.

Spaghetti

1½ cups spaghetti	=	375 ml
1 in. long hot pepper	=	1
¼ tsp. salt and ¼ tsp. pepper		
1 qt. cold water	=	32 ozs.
2 tbsps. butter	=	25 ml
3 tbsps. cheddar cheese	=	25 ml
1 ripe tomato	=	1
Parmesan grated cheese is optional	=	1

Fill a medium-sized pot with 1 or more quarts of water. Let it boil with hot pepper and salt first. Next, put spaghetti in and stir occasionally so it doesn't stick to the bottom. Boil it at 3 o'clock position for about half an hour. If you see that it needs more water, add some more. After it is brought to a boil, taste the spaghetti and see if it is ready. It is better to use a bit more salt in the boiling spaghetti than usual, because it is easier to salt it while it is boiling than salt it after it is drained. Now you are ready to drain spaghetti through the wire mesh. If salt is needed, use it. Now add butter and cheddar cheese and stir with fork while it is still on the stove. Parmesan cheese and tomato juice can be added. Tomato juice squeezed from a garden-grown tomato is the best juice. It gives a real flavor to your spaghetti. Cover with lid and let simmer for 5 minutes. Spaghetti tastes best when served hot or warm. Serves 4.

Roast Beef

2 lbs. beef	= 1 kg.
1 inch long hot pepper	= 1
½ tsp. salt and ½ tsp. pepper	= 2 ml, 2 ml
1 cup water	= 250 g. or 8 ozs.

Carve the meat and around the bone first, then put it in a roasting pan. Add salt and pepper to the meat and hot pepper. Pour water in. Put it in the oven at 325° F = 180° C and let it cook 1 hour in that heat. Then turn the heat to 250° F = 120° C to roast for 3 hours. When tender, remove it from the oven. Why such a small amount of water is used for roast beef is that the meat has enough juice, which it releases while it is cooking. Otherwise you would have so much water in the pan that you would have to put it on top of the stove to dry. After the meat is tender, you can pour a small amount to the juice if you want to use this as gravy for potatoes and chop some onions and let it cook for 5 minutes. Or you can take the meat out, put it in another container, and keep it on top of the stove on low heat just to keep it warm while you are making gravy. Add 1 tablespoon of flour and chopped onions, make batter with a fork. Pour some water into it and stir. See that it is salty enough. If you want some sliced meat in gravy, slice and add it to the gravy and put it back in the oven for about 5 minutes. Note: The flour does not necessarily need to brown to make good gravy. Some cooks burn flour in the frying pan on top of the stove and smoke up the kitchen. Greasy juice can be used for potatoes instead of making gravy. Take it out of the oven and let cool. Serves 6.

• Humans eat less meat than any meat-eating creatures. And yet some are strict vegetarians.

• Humans are only ones that prepare meat for consumption.

Mushrooms with Sauce

1 lb. raw mushrooms	= 454 g.
½ in-long hot pepper	= ½
¼ tsp. salt and ¼ tsp. pepper	= 1 ml, 1 ml
1 qt. water	= 1
1 tbsp. flour	= 15 ml
2 tbsps. oil	= 25 ml
½ onions	= ½
4 cloves garlic	= 4

Put the mushrooms in a pot of 1 quart of water and bring it to a boil. Next, put the sliced mushrooms in and let boil with hot pepper. Add onion, salt and pepper. Boil at 3 o'clock position till they are ready. Cut each clove of garlic in two pieces and let boil 20 to 30 minutes. See that a small amount of water is left, as it is supposed to be thick. In the last 5 or 10 minutes, add oil, flour and juice from the mushrooms and make batter with a fork. Put the batter back into the pot and let it boil. Remove from the heat and let cool. Do not eat it hot! Serves about 6.

Chicken in Gravy

1 chicken	= 1
1 small onion	= 1
½-in. long piece hot pepper	= ½
½ tsp. salt and ½ tsp. pepper	= 2 ml, 2 ml
½ qt. water	= 16 ozs.

Cut the chicken up into about 12 pieces and place them in the pan. Add hot pepper, salt and pepper. Cut the onion up in pieces, and let them boil in a little bit of water, in the oven, in medium heat. In the last 10 minutes, while there is juice and oil left, add some flour to it, stir with a fork, and make batter in the hot pan. The flour doesn't need to brown to make good gravy; it cooks before it browns. It leaves the gravy delicious, not the kind that tastes of burned flour. You can pour some water to make it thinner, as it makes good gravy. Taste and see if there is enough salt. If you taste it too salty, pour some water, stir and let boil for a while. Good to eat with fresh, boiled potatoes. Serves 8.
• Gravies made in the oven have more flavor. As it is not burned and then boiled, it saves its flavor.

Ground Beef

1 lb. ground beef	= 454 g.
¼ tsp. powdered hot pepper	= ¼
½ tsp. salt and ¼ pepper	= 2 ml, 1 ml
1 onion	= 1
4 cloves of garlic	= 4
2 tbsps. flour	= 25 ml

Put the ground beef and spread it on a wide pan. Next, salt and pepper it. Spread a bit of powdered hot pepper on it, with chopped onions and garlic, as well as some flour. Mix it well with a fork. Now it's up to you, whether you want flat beef cakes 3 inches in diameter without gravy while oil and juice from the meat will serve as gravy. You can add some water and let boil. The mixture serves as wonderful gravy substitute. Or you can make small meat balls and make gravy. Add 2 tablespoons of flour to the pan and mix it with a fork making a batter. The flour doesn't have to brown to make good gravy. If short of water, add some and stir occasionally. You can make thin gravy if you want. It's delicious with fresh potatoes. Let it boil for a while. As ground beef cooks faster than other meat, you keep it in the oven 1½ hours at 300° F = 150° C. Serves 6.

Ground Beef or Meat Sausage

1 lb. ground beef or meat sausages	= 454 g.
½ cup chopped onions	= 125 ml
5 cloves garlic	= 5 c.
½ tsp. salt and ¼ tsp. pepper	= 2 ml, 1 ml
1 tsp. mace	= 5 ml
¼ tsp. powdered hot pepper	= 1 ml

Spread the meat out flat on a wide, flat pan. Treat it with salt, pepper and hot powdered pepper. Add the finely chopped onions, mace, and garlic. Mix it well. Now, make it into small balls and put them in a roasting pan. Add a little water if needed and let it cook in the oven at 300° F = 150° C for about an hour. Serves 6.

• If there were no teeth, there would be no need of toothpicks.

Scalloped Potatoes

2 potatoes	=	2
1 onion	=	1
¼ tsp. salt and ¼ tsp. pepper	=	1 ml, 1 ml
¼ tsp. powdered hot pepper	=	1 ml
2 tbsps. cooking oil	=	25 ml
1 cup water	=	250 ml
¼ cup cereal cream or milk	=	60 g.

Slice raw potatoes in thin slices and cut them in two, placing them in roasting pan. Slice an onion thin too. Add salt, pepper, and hot pepper powder. Pour in oil and water, but not too much, as you want the water absorbed completely before you add cereal cream when the potatoes and onions are ready, but have a few minutes left to bring the cream to boil. Let it cook in the roasting pan, in the oven for about 5 minutes till the cream almost dries up. Serves 2.

Sauerkraut with Meat

1½ lbs. short ribs	=	679 g.
2 cups sauerkraut	=	500 ml
½ tbsp. salt and 1 tsp. pepper	=	8 ml, 5 ml
½ inch piece hot pepper	=	½
3 qts. water	=	96 ozs.

Take a big pot, fill it with water, and bring it to a boil. Then put meat in to boil together with hot pepper, salt and pepper. Let it boil at 3 o'clock position. Add sauerkraut in the last half hour. Let it boil till ready. If you prefer it more sour, add some vinegar to it in case the sauerkraut is not sour enough. No onions necessary. Let it cool and serve warm. Serves 6.

• For leftovers, food does not have to be boiled again. Just warm it. It serves well.
• Salt is more easily noticed to the taste than sugar in the same amount, or even much more.
• There are two things that need preparation: Women need to be prepared by men; food needs to be prepared by cooks.

To Boil Pirogies

If you want to boil pirogies, fill the pot with water add a piece of hot pepper and salt, and bring it to a boil. Next, put the pirogies in and let them boil. Stir occasionally, at heat 3 o'clock position, till the pirogies start floating on top. Do not boil them too long, for they will get too soft. Pick them out with a wire spoon, drain well, and put them in another container. Sprinkle salt and pepper over them. Grease them with hot oil, with fried chopped onions and fat crumbs. See that the onions do not burn, but have the fat crumbs well done for better flavor. Now pick the container up and roughen them up so to mix them well in the oil. If your pirogies are made with potato and cheddar cheese, you can add a few spoons of Parmesan cheese crumbs. They are delicious!

To Boil Cabbage Rolls

To boil cabbage rolls, let the water in the pot be brought to a boil with hot pepper, and salt in it. Now pour hot water even with the cabbage rolls. Put the pot in the oven at 325° F = 160° C and let boil till the water almost dries up. Take them out of the oven and grease them with hot oil. No onions are necessary. They are delicious. When there are some leftovers, keep them in a cool place, in the fridge. At the next meal, they need to be heated on an oily frying pan. They are even more delicious when they are heated cold. They are delicious!

Pizza

1 to 1½ cups macaroni	= 250 ml, 375ml
2 tbsps. cheddar cheese	= 25 ml
12 slices sausage	= 12
¼ tsp. salt	= 1 ml
¼ tsp. powdered hot pepper	= 1 ml
2 tbsps. oil	= 25 ml

Have ready, boiled macaroni spread on a dough crust. Add cheddar cheese on top. Add salt and pepper powder. Add sliced sausage on top. Add oil. Use tomato ketchup if preferred. Place the pizza in hot oven at 300° F = 150° C till the crust turns brown. Take it out and let cool. Pizza is best served when hot. Serves 2 or 3.

Garlic Bread

Powdered hot pepper can be added to the flour, while baking bread dough. One half tbsp. of powdered pepper can be added to six loaves of bread dough. Dissolve the powder in hot water first.

Toast

4 slices bread	= 4
4 slices butter	= 4
1/8 tsp. hot powdered pepper	= 0.5 ml

After the bread is toasted on both sides, spread butter over it. You can sprinkle a bit of hot powder pepper, and then smoothen it out with a table knife. Serves 2.

Canned Beets

3 or 4 medium-size beet heads	= 3 to 4
½ cup vinegar	= 125 ml
½ in.- piece hot pepper	= 1
½ tsp. salt	= ½
2 qts water	= 64 ozs.

Slice the skinned, raw beets or cut them into quarters and boil them in water for 2 hours first before you add other ingredients. It is easier to slice beets after you boil them first. Beets are very hard to slice raw and it takes a long time to boil them to get them ready. In the last half hour, add salt and hot pepper and pour vinegar in and let boil till they are soft, 2½ hours altogether. Remove from the heat and let cool. Put them into sealers and place them in cool, dark place. Remember, beets are not good without vinegar. Use them as pickles.

Hot Tea Drink

Bring the water to a boil. Pour 2 cups of boiling water into a teapot with 1¼ teaspoon tea leaves and hot pepper of powder pepper. Let it brew for 5 minutes. Serves 2.

• To prepare food, there are three prime guides: (1) you need a recipe, (2) you need ingredients, (3) you need to prepare it properly.

• Good soup largely depends on good water.

Jellied Fish

1 white fish (2 lbs.)	= 1 kg.
¼ tsp. hot pepper powder	= 1 ml
¼ tsp. salt and ¼ tsp. pepper	= 1 ml, 1 ml
1 small onion	= 1
¼ cup water	= 60 ml

Slice the fish into 2-inch wide pieces, then put it in a roasting pan. Cut the onion into small pieces, and add with it salt and pepper and hot pepper powder. Pour a bit of water and boil it under low heat. First try it on top of the stove, while you can move it around so it doesn't stick to the pan. Pour some oil on it. Now, you can put it in the oven at 300° F = 150° C. After it is half done, turn the fish over to the other side. If there is any water needed, pour on a bit and let it boil for 5 minutes. Why is little water added? Because the fish has a lot of its own juice, which it releases it when it cooks. After it is ready, there is some juice and oil left that can be used as substitute for gravy. It is delicious for boiled, mashed potatoes, or to dip your bread in. Fish and this juicy oil are good with potatoes. Serves 4 to 6.

Fried Liver

Put salt, pepper and hot powder pepper over the liver. Slice 1 large onion and some garlic. Onions can be fried first on the frying pan and then garlic. Take the onions and garlic out, then add more oil to the pan. Next, take a flat container, add some flour, and lay both sides of each slice into the flour. Then put it in the frying pan in medium heat. After both sides are done, turn the heat on very low, then put the fried onions and garlic back into pan, over the liver, cover with a lid and let it simmer for 5 minutes. This is the only time you can have it covered with a lid. When frying at the beginning, it is best to keep it uncovered, so the air will escape, letting the food breathe. If it's fried covered, it will have a strong odor. It serves good with boiled, mashed potatoes. If there are any leftovers, put away in the fridge. Keep it covered, it will soften the meat. The longer it is kept covered in the fridge the more tasty it becomes. It softens and becomes quite delicious. If 1 pound of liver is prepared, it will serve about 4.

• Potatoes stay preserved longer than any vegetables. Yet they deteriorate faster after they are boiled.

Cured Bacon

3½ lbs. bacon	= 1.5 kg.
3 tbsps. salt	= 45 ml
½ tsp. hot powdered pepper	= 3 ml

Get a slab of bacon, salt it, and sprinkle hot pepper powder. Next, wrap it up in waxed paper and put it in a cold place, near the freezer, so it doesn't freeze but stays cold. Use waxed paper for wrapping. Avoid brown manila paper as it forms an odor. Make holes in the waxed paper. Let it season for 3 or 4 weeks, till it gets cured. It is important to make holes in the bacon so that the salt can get inside as well.

Dried, Salt Fish

After the fish is cleaned, salt the fish all around. Use powdered hot pepper the same way. Let fish stay for a few weeks in the fridge before it is ready.

Fried Fish

Slice the fish in 1¼-inch wide pieces. Sprinkle salt, pepper, and hot pepper powder the same way. Take a pan of flour and coat both sides of each piece, then put them in a hot, greasy frying pan. Do not cover the frying pan with a lid when frying, but let the moisture escape and leave them dry. This also will allow the odor to escape and allow it to breathe. Notice that no onions are needed. Serve with boiled, mashed potatoes.

Seasoned Butter

To season butter with powdered hot pepper, first, soften the butter in a warm kitchen. Flatten the butter and sprinkle it with hot powder pepper, mix it well with a fork, then make it into a lump as it used to be. Let it stay for a few days. Good for all uses.

• Never salt meat like bacon so it will stay for a few weeks. Meat can lose its flavor.

• Hunger alone makes for the best taste. Its taste is above many ingredients.

Fried Sweet Cream

½ cup sweet cream (fresh country unpasteurized)	= 125 ml
¼ cup fine chopped onions	= 10 ml
1/8 tsp. hot pepper powder	= 0.5 ml
1/8 tsp. salt and 1/8 pepper	= 0.5 ml, 0.5 ml

Now we'll go to the country to do country cooking, where fresh cream can be easily gotten from cows. Take a frying pan, and first pour in only ¼ of a cup. Then add finely chopped onions to the cream, and let fry on low heat for 5 minutes. Now slice the cold, boiled potatoes and put them into the pan. Add salt, pepper, and hot pepper powder. Let heat. You can add the rest of the cream and let heat. If more salt is needed, add some. Eggs can be fried on cream too. More foods can be fried on oil than on cream. Cream is one that is the more delicious. Cream shrinks and turns faster to oil under heat. That is why a little more is added to the food. Eggs can be fried on sweet cream. They are very delicious . Serves 2.

Fried Lamb or Pork Chops

4 chops (lamb or pork)	= 4
Salt and pepper	
Hot pepper powder	

Carve the meat and around the bones. Sprinkle the meat on both sides with salt and peppers. Now put them in a hot frying pan, resting on the fat side and let the fat fry first. Have both sides fry till they are brown. Serves 2.

• Lamb and pork come with a different taste and with a different color.

• Potatoes are the most difficult foods to prepare properly and make them delicious. Potatoes are stubborn; they can be good with proper preparation.

Jellied Chicken

1 chicken	= 1
1 onion	= 1
½ tsp. salt and ½ tsp. pepper	= 3 ml
½ in. long hot pepper	= ½
2 qts. water	= 64 ozs.

Cut up the chicken into small pieces and put it in the pot of already boiled water. Cut the onion into 6 to 8 pieces. Put it all in together with salt and the pepper. Let it boil at 3 o'clock position. When it gets soft, turn off the heat. See that it retains enough water (small amount), so that when it jellies, it is thick enough. If the jelly is softer than for head cheese, it will do. You can either leave it in the pot to cool, partially uncovered, or put it into sealers. Store away in cool, dark place. Or it can be put into sealers and put in the canner and let boil at medium heat. See that the canner is filled with water 2 inches above the sealers. The sealers can be put in first, then warm water can be poured in.

Dill Pickles

Small cucumbers	
Garlic	= 4 c.
Salt (2 tsps.)	= 10 ml
Hot pepper (1 tsp.)	= 5 ml
Water (2 qts.)	= 64 ozs.
Dill weed or seed (½ tsp.)	= 3 ml

For 2 qt. sealers, fill with cucumbers. Add 2 cloves of garlic to each sealer. Add 1 tsp. salt to 1½ qts. of water. Half-inch piece of hot pepper, 1 tsp. salt. 1 tsp. dill seed. Garlic can be added raw to cucumbers in sealers. Put the cucumbers into the sealers. Then add salt, hot pepper, and dill weed and let it boil for 5 minutes. Take it off the stove and let cool till warm. Then pour into sealers where the cucumbers already are. Seal tight and store it in a cool, dark place.

• There is no drink more tasteless than water. Since water is tasteless, it will only taste good when you are thirsty.

Pickles

10 green tomatoes	= 10
3 small onions	= 3
1½ qts. water	= 48 ozs.
½ tsp. hot pepper powder	= 3 ml
1 tsp. salt	= 5 ml
2 tbsps. brown sugar	= 25 ml
3 tbsps. cinnamon	= 45 ml
1 cup vinegar	= 250 ml

Slice the tomatoes and onions and put them into a pot of water. Add all the rest of the ingredients in a separate pot and let boil for 5 minutes. The 5 minutes of boiling helps to bring them all together, though tomatoes and onions are supposed to be left raw meantime. Now, put all ingredients into one pot, and let boil for 5 minutes. Then, pour into sealers and seal tight. Store in a cool, dark place.

Onion Pickles

Pick out small, white onions and peel them. Carve each one with a knife and put them in the pot. Add 1 cup of vinegar to 3 quarts of onions. Add 2 tablespoons brown sugar, 2 tablespoons of cinnamon, ½ teaspoon of hot pepper powder, 1 teaspoon of salt and pour water. Have all in the pot and let it boil for 5 minutes. Let it cool a bit, then pour into the sealers and seal. Store it in cool, dark place.

Pickled Cauliflower

2 lbs. cauliflower	= 1 kg.
1½-in. hot pepper	= 1½
1 tsp. salt	= 5 ml
1 tbsp. dill seed	= 15 ml

Cut the cauliflower into desired pieces and put them in the pot together with other ingredients. Now, let it boil for 5 minutes. Then pour into sealers and seal. Keep it in a warm place. It takes 3 or 4 weeks to season. After awhile, put it in a cool, dark place.

Pickled Carrots

6 carrots (young)	= 6
½ tsp. hot pepper powder	= 3 ml
½ tsp. salt	= 3 ml
1 tbsp. dill seed	= 8 ml
2 qts water	= 64 ozs.

Pick 6 young carrots and cut them in two. Put them into the pot together with the rest of the ingredients, and let it boil till the carrots get soft. Next, put them into the sealers, and seal. Keep them in a warm place. Let it season for 3 or 4 weeks.

Stuffed Buns

1 lb dough	= 454 g.
½ lb. ground beef	= 227 g.
¼ tsp. salt and ¼ tsp. pepper	= 1 ml, 1 ml
¼ tsp. hot pepper powder	= 1 ml
½ cup fine chopped onions, green or white	= 125 ml

Get a pound of dough that is prepared for baking bread. Cut into small buns, spread them open. Prepare the filling by having the ground beef ready cooked. Mix other ingredients with the meat. Use this as filling. Roll up the dough, making the buns into balls. Put them into a pan and put them in the hot oven at 300° F till they get brown. They should serve several people.

Stuffed Poultry

Take a clean chicken and salt and pepper it in- and outside. Prepare basic stuffing with 2 or 3 slices of bread made into bread crumbs. Add 1/3 finely chopped onions to 2/3 of bread crumbs. Add salt and pepper and a bit of oil over the bread crumbs. Sprinkle with water to make the crumbs moist. Mix well. Use the hot pepper powder only on the outside of the chicken. Put this stuffing into the chicken. Push in but not tight. Sew the opening. Put it in the roasting pan, pour a bit of water. The reason not to pour too much water is that the poultry has a lot of its own juice, so when it is roasting, it releases a lot of juice. First fry it on top of the stove on low heat, and on the bottom, moving the poultry around so it doesn't stick to the bottom of the pan, adding a little water. Then put it in the oven at 325°F = 160°C, and let roast till ready. You would need to turn the chicken over. You will notice that it releases a lot of juice and it's full of water. When that happens at the end, you take it out and put it on top of the stove over low heat, let it dry out, then put it back in the oven to finish up. In case you have some leftovers of the dressing, you can add it to the roasting pan in the last 15 minutes. See that it is mixed with juice. It should be enough to serve the family.

Rib Roast

1 lb. ribs	=	454 g.
1 small onion	=	1
¼ tsp. hot pepper powder	=	1 ml
¼ tsp. salt and ¼ tsp. pepper	=	1 ml, 1 ml
1 to 2 cups water	=	250 ml, 500 ml
4 cloves garlic (optional) Fine! Add it in the last 20 minutes	=	4 c.

Put the ribs in the roasting pan. Pour some water, add salt, pepper and hot pepper. Add an onion (carved) to it. Put it in the oven at 325° F = 160° C. and let it cook till it is ready. Some cooks may include a few vegetables like carrots and potatoes to cook with it. But the vegetables happen to take the taste away from the meat, and the real flavor is not with the meat. Of course, the vegetables may have more flavor. The option is with the cooks whether they want to mix vegetables with meat or not. You can add 4 cloves of garlic to the rib roast in the last 15 minutes. Have them cut in 2 or 3 pieces. If you want to make gravy, see that it contains enough water and oil. If there isn't enough, add some. It should taste very good with boiled, mashed potatoes. Serves 6.

• Never fry or boil frozen meat or fish, for it reduces flavor. Let it thaw completely first. Partially frozen meat is the easiest to cut or carve.

• By allowing the frozen meat to thaw and allowing the blood from the meat and juice to come on top, it retains better flavor.

Seasoning, Meat Roast

2 lbs. beef	= 1 kg.
¼ tsp. hot pepper powder	= 1 ml
½ tsp. salt and ¼ tsp. pepper	= 1 ml, 1 ml
1 tbsp. vinegar	= 15 ml

Get 2 pounds of beef and carve the meat so the ingredients you then treat it with will get inside as well. Now, wrap the meat in waxed paper, and put it in the fridge, just under the freezer, so it doesn't freeze too much, and let it stay overnight. The next day, put it in the roasting pan, with some water, and let it roast in the oven at 325° F. Let it roast for half an hour then turn the heat down to 300° F = 150° C. Under slow cooking it should be ready in 3 to 3½ hours. Take it out of the oven. It could serve from 8 to 10 people, served with other things at the meal.

Hot Pepper Plum Fruit

2 lbs. plums	= 1 kg.
½ tsp. hot pepper powder	= 3 ml
½ cup sugar	= 125 ml
1 qt. water	= 32 ozs.

Take 2 pounds of prune plums. Wash them. Soak them in a pot of water. Add all the ingredients to it, and let stand overnight. See that water is even with the fruit. Let it boil till you notice the fruit is soft. One thing, you don't need too much water in the fruit. You'd rather have the juice strong. After they cool, put them into the sealers and seal tight. Store it away in a cool, dark place. You will notice hot pepper will not taste strong in the fruit, because the fruit absorbs the flavor of the pepper, although, it is there all the same.

Raw Potato Patties

2 raw potatoes	=	2
¼ tsp. hot pepper powder	=	1 ml
¼ tsp. salt and ¼ tsp. pepper	=	1 ml, 1 ml
½ onion	=	½
2 tbsps. flour	=	25 ml

Cut the potatoes into pieces and grind them fine through a blender. Do the same with onions. Add to this hot pepper powder, salt and pepper. Add flour to it as well. Mix it well with a fork, and start making small balls, flattening them. Now they're ready for the frying pan. More oil is needed to fry raw potato patties than mashed potato patties, and it takes longer to fry them. Put them on a wide pan with enough oil. Turn them over to get the other side done as well, by adding some more oil to the pan. They are good served hot. Serves 2.

Pickled Hard-Boiled Eggs

12 eggs

Take a dozen small eggs, boil them in a pot of water for 5 or 6 minutes. Take them out and let cool. Peel them and put them into sealers. Take another pot of water and put in the rest of the ingredients. Chop onion fine, add 2 cloves of chopped garlic, salt and both peppers. Add 2 tablespoons of vinegar. More vinegar can be added if preferred. Add 1 quart of water to the pot. Let it boil for 5 minutes. Pour it into the sealers where the eggs already are. Seal and store in a cool, dark place.

Spaghetti and Meat Balls

1 lb. ground beef	= 454 g.
½ cup spaghetti (cooked)	= 125 ml
½ cup onions	= 125 ml
4 cloves garlic	= 4
Salt and pepper	
2 tbsps. flour	= 25 ml
Water	

Spread out the meat flat, sprinkle with salt, and pepper. Add fine chopped onions and garlic. Mix it well and start making small balls (including the boiled spaghetti). Put them in a roasting pan, pour some water into it, and put the pan in the oven at 300° F = 150° C. And let cook till the meat is soft. Add about 2 tablespoons of flour to the oil and juice and mix it with a fork, adding more water if needed. Stir well and occasionally till the flour almost turns brown. Do not use too much flour or it won't be the same flavor as it should be. The gravy can be made thin by pouring some more water into it, as gravy gets thick later. It depends on how much juice and oil there is. Then you can add flour to make plenty of gravy. If gravy is not required, add only a small amount of water to meat balls. This should be good with boiled, mashed potatoes. Serves 6.

Spaghetti Squares

½ lb. flour	= 247 g.
½ cup warm water	= 125 ml
½ tsp. salt	= 2 ml
1 onion	= 1
4 cloves garlic	= 4
3 tbsps. oil	= 45 ml
¼ tsp. hot pepper =1 ml	
3 tbsps. cheddar cheese	= 45 ml

Take the flour, add salt to it, and mix well. Pour water into flour and mix it with a fork. Try to make the dough the same as if you were making it for pirogies. Flatten the dough after you get it of the right consistency. Add a bit of flour to the dough so it won't stick to the rolling pan. Roll the dough flat, then take a knife, and cut it into 2-inch strips. Then cut it crosswise 2 inches. Have the water boiling. Now put these into the water and stir occasionally with a wide wooden spoon. It shouldn't get them long to get ready, as the dough is fairly soft, not like dry spaghetti. After they start floating on top, they are ready. Take them out with a screen separator, drain well, and put in another container. After you have the onions and garlic fried in oil in the frying pan with salt and the peppers in, take a large spoon and pour it over the spaghetti, while it is still hot. If you want to, you can add the oil alone to the spaghetti, flopping them to see they are well oiled. Use fried onions and garlic sparingly or none at all. Next, add 3 teaspoons of cheddar cheese and spread it all over the spaghetti. Or you can omit onions and garlic. Just add 2 tbsps. of butter and cheddar cheese. Cover with a lid and let simmer for 5 minutes. Adding enough oil and cheese to spaghetti, makes them more delicious. A work of caution: when putting spaghetti into boiling water, see that you don't have the heat on too high, because the water rises with foam on top because there is loose flour on the dough. Have it lowered for a while, then raise the heat higher around the 3 o'clock position. Serves 6.

Liver Hamburger

½ lb. liver	= 247 g.
1 onion	= 1
4 cloves garlic	= 4
2 tbsps flour	= 25 ml
Salt and pepper	= 0.5 ml, 0.5 ml
Several tbsps. oil	

Have enough oil in frying pan. Chop onions and garlic and fry till brown. Put onions first, because onions fry longer than garlic. Garlic happens to burn before onions start to brown. After this is done, take a spoon with holes in it, and take all the fried onions and garlic out, leaving the oil in the pan. You may add more oil to fry the liver. Now take a flat pan with some flour in it. Salt and pepper the liver on both sides, and put them in hot frying pan, frying both sides well. After this is done, put the onions and garlic on top of the liver, cover with a lid, and let simmer for 5 minutes. Would serve good with boiled, hot mashed potatoes. Eat it while it is still hot. Serves 6.

Beef Fat Crumb Fried Eggs

1 tbsp. beef fat crumbs	= 15 ml
2 eggs	= 2
Salt and pepper	= 0.5 ml, 0.5 ml

Cut the beef fat into small crumbs and fry them on the frying pan till they turn brown. Leave enough oil for frying. This fat may have already been seasoned in salt. Fry 2 eggs. Add salt and the peppers. Take a large spoon and bring the hot oil over the eggs till the yokes turn white. Good to serve with potatoes. Serves 1.

Chicken Livers and Hearts, Etc., Sauce

¼ lb. livers	= 125 g.
¼ lb. hearts	= 125 g.
¼ lb. gizzards	= 125 g.
½ tsp. salt	= 3 ml
¼ tsp. pepper	= 1 ml
¼ tsp. hot pepper powder	= 1 ml
1 qt. water	= 32 ozs.
1 small onion	= 1
4 cloves garlic	= 4

Put the meat and carved onion, salt, and peppers in a roasting pan with 1 quart of water, and put it in an oven at 300° F = 150° C. You can add garlic whole, in the last 15 minutes. Garlic doesn't have to be too soft. It can be left when it gets to soften. In this way, it can retain its flavor. It shouldn't take very long to get it ready, as it is quite soft. About 1 hour may be sufficient. When it's ready, add about 2 tablespoons of flour, and make batter with a fork. If more water is needed, add some and stir. Let it cook for 5 minutes. This makes it like gravy. Good when served with boiled, hot mashed potatoes. Serves up to 6.

Beans with Bacon

3 tbsps. beans	= 45 ml
3 slices bacon	= 3
Salt and pepper	
slight dash hot pepper powder	= 0.5 ml
2 tbsps. flour	= 25 ml
1 small onion	= 1
2 to 4 cloves of garlic	= 2
2 cups water	= 500 ml

After you have beans soaking for 6 to 8 hours put them to boil first in a small pot, on top of the stove for about 2 hours. Add bacon, salt, and pepper in the last 1 hour. After it is near ready, take some flour and make batter with a fork in a small amount of juice that is left and mix it well. Next, bring it to a boil for 5 minutes, stirring occasionally so the flour does not stick to the bottom of the pot. Serves well with boiled, mashed potatoes and with a few other things you choose. Serves 2.

Hot French Toast

2 eggs	= 2
½ cup milk or cereal cream	= 125 ml
1/8 tsp. hot pepper powder	= 0.5 ml
¼ tsp. powdered garlic	= 1 ml
Several slices of bread	

Put first four ingredients into 1 container and use an egg beater; stir it well. If the mixture is thin, you can make more toast. But if it's thick, you will have less. Get a wide frying pan and add a bit of oil. Have it on the stove on medium heat. Put both soaked sides of bread slices in the batter, place it in the oily pan and fry one side at a time. Each time you put in new slices, you have to add oil to the frying pan. Keep adding slices till you use up the batter. Serves 2 or 3.

Seasoned Butter

1 lb. butter	= 454 g.
1 tsp. garlic powder	= 5 ml
1/8 tsp. hot pepper powder	= 0.5 ml

Put the butter in a container, and let it soften to room temperature. Use these ingredients and mix them in the butter. Next, try to put the butter back in shape. Wrap it in wax paper and store it in the fridge. It should be good for all uses.

• Garlic is stronger to taste, but it doesn't retain flavor like onions after cooking; garlic retains odor longer.

Beef Stew with Rice

1 lb. stewing beef	=	500 g.
1 onion	=	1
½-inch long hot pepper	=	½
1 tsp. salt and ½ tsp. pepper	=	5 ml, 3 ml
1 cup rice	=	250 ml
4 cloves garlic	=	4
1 tbsp. oil	=	15 ml
2 qts. water	=	64 ozs.

Let stewing beef boil together with all the ingredients, except onions and garlic. Add the whole, carved onion. In the last 15 minutes, add garlic, cut in 2 pieces. Let it boil at 3 o'clock position, till most of the water dries up, just a bit of juice is left. Boil rice in a separate pot and drain the water out, leaving rice dry. Now add rice to beef stew, add salt and oil, stir it up. If beef is in large pieces, cut it into small pieces. Cover with a lid and let simmer for 5 minutes. Good to serve with boiled, mashed potatoes and a few other foods you have. Serves 6 to 8.

Meat Rolls

Take about ½ pound of dough, the kind that has been prepared for baking bread. Roll it out thin with a rolling pen (leaving the dough soft). Spread over with mixture of ground beef, chopped onions, salt and both peppers. (Use hot pepper powder sparingly for this kind of a meal.) Next, roll up the dough as if you would make cinnamon rolls. Now cut it into 1¼-inch wide pieces and put them in a wide pan about 1 inch apart, and put them in the oven at 300° F = 150° C till they rise and brown. Now they should rise and be all together. Take them out and let cool. Should yield about 2 dozen. It is well to treat ground beef with salt and peppers, and fine chopped onions; mix well first. Next, spread over the dough.

Treated Sausage or Bologna

Take ½ lb. of sausage and slice it into half-inch slices. Put the pieces into a frying pan and add a bit of water. Add a bit of hot pepper powder, a bit of salt, and let boil for 5 minutes. The reason salt is used is that the water may take away some of the salt from the meat. The same can be done with the bologna. Serves 6.

THREE
NON-HOT PEPPER RECIPES

Beet-Leaf Rolls

Large amount beet leaves that will do for the whole pot	= ½ pot leaves
A container thick dough that will do enough (I can't specify just how much leaves and dough)	= ¼ pot dough
1 tbsp. salt	= 15 ml
1 tsp. pepper	= 5 ml
2 qts. water	= 64 ozs.
2 tbsps. oil	= 25 ml
2 tbsps. sour cream to 1 plate	= 25 ml

Pick a large amount of tender beet leaves. Wash them carefully a few times, so there will be no dirt. With large leaves, cut them in two in the middle of the leaf. Prepare some thick dough. Take some on the spoon and spread it over each leaf, thin along the leaf. Then roll up the leaf with filling in, starting from one end to the other to make them look like cabbage rolls. As you are making them, put them into the pot one by one. It is well to put some leaves on the bottom of the pot first, so they don't stick to the bottom. Old leaves would do for this. After you have filled the pot with rolls, do not press them down too tight, for they will set themselves while they are cooking. Rice can be used for filling. But first, soak the rice for several hours to soften. Made with dough taste better with sour cream. Make dough for filling just medium thick. Add salt and pepper and a bit of oil to rice, but do not add any oil or pepper to dough. Do not add any oil to the rolls before boiling them. After the pot is filled, water even with the top of the rolls. Add salt and pepper, then cover with the leaves so they don't dry on top. During cooking in the oven, they will set about 1/3. So here you will have a full pot. Put it in the oven at 325° F = 160° C. Let them cook till they are ready. See that the water doesn't dry and leave them burning. After they are ready, you want about 2 inches of water left on the bottom in the pot. With this the rolls will keep moist. Otherwise, they will be dry. But for cabbage rolls, it is better to have it dry on the end. After they are ready, take the pot out of the oven, take the lid off, partially, and let the air out. Then you can use soft butter on top or heated oil from the frying pan. Set some on a plate or plates and add sour cream on top. (Farmer's cream is the best.) They are delicious and healthy. After the meal is over, put the rest away in the fridge with lid partially covered. For leftovers, during the next meal, they don't need to be heated like cabbage rolls. Just add sour cream on top and eat them cold. Perhaps they could taste better cold. They could serve about 6.

Stuffed Fish

1 fish (any kind)	= 1
½ tsp. salt and ¼ tsp. pepper	= 3 ml, 1 ml
2 slices bread crumbs	= 2
2 to 3 tbsps. oil	= 25 ml, 45 ml
1/3 onion (chopped very fine)	= 1/3

Clean the fish and soak it in water. Take it out and salt and pepper it all over. Prepare bread crumbs. Add salt and pepper, oil and sprinkle with water (do not make it too wet). Mix it well. Add chopped onions to it. Stuff fish loosely, but not tight. Put the fish into the roasting pan. Add about 2 tablespoons of oil to the pan. Do not use any water for the pan, as the fish has a lot of juice in it and will release it when cooking. First, begin frying on top of stove, turning the fish so it doesn't stick to the bottom of the pan. Then put it in the oven at 300° F = 150° C, checking to see that it is not sticking. The fish will need to be turned over after it been cooking for about half an hour. It should be ready in 1 hour. You will find enough juice in the pan and it is very delicious with boiled, hot mashed potatoes. Should serve up to 6. Good eating.

• This is where most of the onions go into the food, for stuffing a fish or poultry. Even though it has strong flavor, you won't notice it much after it is roasted.

• No garlic for fish or poultry stuffing.

40

Stuffed Green Peppers

4 green peppers	= 4
½ cup rice	= 125 ml
¼ tsp. salt and ¼ tsp. pepper	= 1 ml, 1 ml
1 tbsp. oil	= 15 ml
½ cup water	= 125 ml

First, cut the peppers on the edge and take the seeds out. Stuff it with soaked rice, salted and oiled, with some chopped onions together. Put these in the roasting pan. Add water and oil to it and put it in an oven at 300° F = 150° C for about 1 hour. Take them out and serve the food you like. Serves 4 people.

Sliced Cucumbers and Onions

3 cucumbers	= 3
1 onion	= 1
Salt (pinch of salt)	= 0.5 ml
2 tbsps. vinegar	= 25 ml

Take a few young cucumbers and 1 onion and slice them. Then put them flat on the platter. Salt them and sprinkle vinegar over them. For this preparation, you use 1/3 of onions to 2/3 of cucumbers. The skin on the cucumbers can be shaved off, but since they are so tender, they can be left on. You will find them crisp; but if you want them to stay in salt and vinegar for several hours and have them softened, they taste better that way. They are better eaten with bread. Serves 2 or 3.

• You can eat more foods with potatoes than any other vegetables, but yet, you can eat more foods with bread than with potatoes.

• Onions (raw) are as medicine to a cold in a nose.

Miniature Cabbage Rolls

3 brussel sprouts	= 3
3 tsps. rice	= 15 ml
Salt and pepper (pinch)	
1 tsp. oil	= 5 ml
1¼ cups water	= 310 ml

Take 3 brussel sprouts and cut each one on the side of the stem. Put them in hot water and let them soak to loosen the leaves. Have soaked rice prepared, salted, and peppered, and oiled. Next, start making cabbage rolls by putting a bit of rice on each leaf and roll the leaf up, just like you would be making cabbage rolls. Before putting them in a little pot, put some leaves on the bottom so they don't burn while cooking. And after you have finished making them, cover the top with more leaves. Add salt and water to the pot, cover with a lid, and put it in an oven at 300° F = 150° C and cook for 1 hour. Take them out and treat them with heated oil. They're really not prepared for a meal, but when you want to kick a party, inviting guests for a meal, set them on the table and greet them with some unique and unexpected serving. If they want to know how to make them, give them a recipe.

Oven-Baked Potatoes

2 large potatoes	= 2
Salt and pepper (1 tsp.)	= 5 ml
2 tbsps. butter	= 25 ml

Wash the potatoes and slice them. Apply lots of salt and some pepper over them. Now put them on a wide pan after melting the butter in it and put them in the oven at 300° F = 150° C till they brown and get full and soft inside. When ready, pick them out and place them in a container. They are good for a snack or eat them with sauerkraut and meat. Since potatoes need only a little salt, this is the time they need the most. Serves 2. If this amount of salt is used for boiled potatoes, it would make them too salty. But for this oven baked, they are just right.

* A potato is about the only one among the vegetables that is the hottest after it's cooked, and it probably cools off the quickest.

Preparing Potatoes

2 large potatoes	= 2
Salt and pepper	= to taste
Several tbsps. butter or oil (2 tbsps.)	= 25 ml
Onions	= 2 slices

Peel the potatoes and cut them into 1½-inch squares. Put them in a pot of water, 1½ inches over the potatoes. Add ½ teaspoon of salt, and let boil till they are ready. Some cooks have been preparing potatoes for years and they still don't know to prepare them well. It is known that potatoes are the hardest foods to prepare well. If you don't follow the rules, they will not taste as good as they should. I would suggest some of the rules here as follows: Have the right size pot for the number of potatoes. For instance, if there are 2 potatoes, have a small-size pot. Fill the pot 2 inches below the top. Do not fill a large-size pot half full. For better flavor, the size of a pot also makes a difference as well as in the manner of preparation. It is known that covering the pot with the lid keeps the heat in, and they boil better. But it is also important for cooking food requires it to breathe (mixing air). So for this, it is required to keep the lid off the pot or have it partially uncovered, allowing the steam to come out, and, at the same time allowing the food to get in contact with fresh air.

It's been heard that cooking outdoors made food taste better. So some of that can be done indoors, as well by following the right rules. There are a few things to remember: do not boil potatoes too rapidly or slowly over low heat. If you cut them into small pieces and boil them rapidly, they will get too soft and lose their flavor. They become sort of starchy. For better flavor, it is better to boil them in big pieces. For good results, have them cut into 1½-inch size and boil them in an open pot. When they become soft, drain the water out and put them back on the stove again on very low heat to dry the remaining water. Do not let them dry too much. They are allowed to get dry, but as well, do not leave too much moisture in them by taking them off the heat. You know what happens. Leaving too much moisture and then mashing them and then drying the moisture from them is not as good as having remaining moisture dry before they are mashed. For better results and for better flavor, do not use a potato masher, but use a fork and poke them, breaking them up. This allows the air to escape and leaves them fresh, but keeps them warm. Allow them to dry some more, then salt and pepper them. Add several tbsps. of butter to 2 potatoes or would you rather have fried chopped onions in butter or in oil? They can taste good enough by adding butter to them alone. Mix it well with the fork. Note: enough oil added to them makes them delicious. If you make them dry, they will have no flavor. They are good tasting when they are prepared well. Potatoes are important. They just can't be overlooked. You have to deal with them. Potatoes are very simple, once they are boiled or fried. They cannot be reboiled or refried or they will lose their flavor, unlike some other foods. Yet, when certain food is prepared, they were boiled two times and fried once, and they were delicious! One thing must be remembered: the potato is "The Most Incredible Vegetable." If you study, you will learn it is the king of the vegetables! After you had potatoes boiled in the pot, when you pick a piece of a potato out from the water, out of the pot to eat it tastes quite good without salt and it is still wet. But after you drain them and salt them they are not as tasty. The flavor seems to go away.

Unpeeled Potatoes

6 medium-size potatoes	= 6
1 tbsp. salt	= 15 ml
2 qts. water	= 64 ozs.

Fill the large pot with water, let it boil at 3 o'clock position. Put the potatoes in. Boil till they are ready. Potatoes with skins can boil at high heat with no foam. Corn, as well, can be boiled at high heat, covered with a lid, with no foam forming. Boil potatoes 35–40 minutes. At this heat, it doesn't matter because the potatoes are in skin and whole. They will keep their flavor. After they are ready, drain them and let them dry. Remove from stove and let cool. Later, for the next meal, you can take some and peel them, slice them up and fry them on an oily frying pan till they brown. Serve them hot with other food you have. The way they were boiled, whole and in skins, they contain a lot of flavor. Delicious! Serves 4 to 6.

• When potatoes freeze, thaw them before boiling. They are still good. Once the potatoes freeze, keep them frozen to preserve them, otherwise they will deteriorate. They are one of the quickest vegetables to deteriorate. Freeze them only once, not the second time.

Boiled Corn

6 ears of corn	= 6 ears
1 tbsp. salt	= 15 ml

Take a large pot and fill it with water. Add salt and bring to a boil. Put in the ears of corn. Boil corn at high heat with a closed lid for 50 minutes; 1 hour if you want it more tender. When the corn is tender enough, drain the water or remove the corn from the water. Next, place the corn in a roasting pan. Add salt and butter to taste. Add water to the bottom of the pan and place it in the over on low heat for 10 minutes. Serves 3 to 6.

FOUR
COUNTRY-STYLE COOKING

Hot-Ash Baked Potatoes

Pick out small potatoes, which are the best to cook in hot ashes. First, make a bonfire till you get enough ashes. Put the potatoes in and cover them with ashes. Keep them in hot ashes till the skin burns dark and they soften inside. This can be done while you are working in the garden, digging and picking potatoes. You will be surprised to find them very tasty with little preparation, even without salt and butter. This is the only time they can be eaten without salt. And just remember, those that are cooked in the oven were treated with the most salt that potatoes cannot take other ways. Prepared both ways they are really delicious! Some workers take time for coffee or for a smoke, but some decide to take time off for a snack barbecuing potatoes. Relax.

Salt-Cured Bacon

Purchase a slab of bacon with more fat, which has hardly any lean. Salt it well. Let it roll in the salt while it is wet. Now wrap it up in waxed paper, and put it under the freezer so it doesn't get frozen for a few days. Later, put it in to freeze or in a cold storage if you have one, such as a cold shed where it will freeze and keep it there for 3 or 4 weeks. It should be ready to slice and use it. The reason it has to be cured this way at home, is that they don't sell it this way in stores, cured or salted this way, like they used to in the olden days. When it's seasoned this way, it preserves the bacon and makes it very delicious as well. This is the way they preserved bacon long ago when they didn't have fridges. This method is mostly forgotten, as well as this delicious taste is also forgotten and young generations never knew it. Now you still can cure bacon the "old-fashioned way" right in your own home. One way is by following a recipe. This recipe will be a constant reminder.

• Liver is the only meat not to be covered with a lid when it is frying, for it will smell foul. It has to breathe (exchange air). The only time it can be covered is when it is put away in the fridge. It will soften it and make it even more delicious.

Smoked Fish

Take some fresh fish and clean and cut them in two. Salt and hang them to be smoked. If you have an old shack, you can use it for this purpose. It doesn't have to be big. A small place is better. How to make smoke? Do not light fires. Just make a fire to smolder from wood. Hanging fish on a nail or by a hook around the tail, they should be secured enough for them to stay hanged. You can leave the skin on. Afterward, you can peel it off, when eating. After they are through, store them away in a cool, dark place. Smoked fish can be fried on an oily frying pan. Do not boil it. Have a good day!

Fried Eggs on Sweet Cream

2 eggs	= 2
¼ cup sweet cream	= 60 ml
Salt and pepper	= pinch

Take a small frying pan and add some sweet cream. Put it on a low heat when frying eggs. The city doesn't have sweet cream like they do on the farm, so let's take a trip to the farm and get some (one goes alone), perhaps do some cooking there. First, have the pan hot with cream already frying. Now fry the eggs. Add salt and pepper, and let fry till the yokes turn white and a little harder if you want them well done. Delicious with potatoes! Those who have lived all their life in the city, don't know what a good tasting egg is, especially when prepared the "country-style" way. Serves you right. Serves 1.

• You know onions are ready, when they start to brown. But it is not necessary to brown garlic to get it ready. Onions still retain flavor after they are fried, but garlic loses its flavor. To retain flavor, it is best to let it fry to half-raw. The sense of smell is more sensitive and stronger than taste to these flavors.

• Onions are the only vegetable that will smoke into your eyes and make the tears run down and the smoke gets into your nose and makes the nose run. Onions have that smoke that you cannot see. Its smoke is stronger than real smoke of a forest fire.

Green Weed Sauce

½ small pot green weed tops	=	½
½ pot water	=	½
½ tsp. salt	=	2 ml
1 tbsp. flour	=	15 ml
2 tbsps. oil	=	25 ml
½ small onion	=	½

The first few months of the summer are the best time of the year to pick green weed tops or leaves, when they are still tender. They grow out over fields and gardens. They are easily noticed; they are green and have white dots. Pick enough of these weeds, leaving the stems out. Wash them a few times in clean water. Since the tops are small, they don't need to be cut. Just put them whole in boiling water. Add salt and boil for about 5 minutes. They get soft in a hurry. Before you put them to boil, add some fine chopped onions. Do not have too much water, because you want to have a bit of juice left to make sauce. Add oil to the sauce. Take some flour and juice from the pot and make batter with a fork. Do not scald the flour with juice. Put it back into the pot, stir and bring to a boil. At mealtime, put some into a saucer and eat with a meal, with a spoon, especially with potatoes, which are best. It is like spinach. After it boils, it becomes less in the pot than it was at first. Word of caution: Nowadays they usually spray fields to combat insects. It isn't safe to pick them unless you're sure they are the right ones. They must be washed. Serves about 4.

• These plants to the farmer are plain weeds, which the farmer tries to get rid of by hard work and by the sweat of his brow.

• Some weeds may get up to here for some farmers and gardeners, but they are still good to eat. Man may not be able to create a single thing for eating but the lowliest plants in the field are good to eat.

Smoked Meat

It looks as if we are going to the country again, this time to smoke meat. Pick out a shack free from any holes and use it to smoke meat. First, cut the beef or pork to a several-pounds size flat, free from bones. Have wood to burn in a fireplace and let it smolder instead of burning. Hang the meat above the smoldering fire. Keep the meat in smoke for at least a week. You can salt the meat well before smoking it. This will not only give you good taste, but something different. There is no use overdoing it, that is having it smoked too much. To separate bacon from pork, cut it up into slabs. Salt the bacon well, and hang it up to be smoked. Or you would rather have the bacon salted only and treat it in smoke for a while? You can do that. The meat is better treated with smoke when it is hanging. Smoke gets all around it. This can be called a shack without a chimney. The best time to do this work is in the fall or in the spring. The heat hasn't a chance to spoil it, or the cold hasn't a chance to freeze it. Frozen meat hasn't a way to be treated by smoke. A mild winter is a good time to smoke meat, as there is no heat or cold to interfere with smoking. After the smoking is finished, store away the meat in a cold, dark place. As for the bones, it's not good to smoke them. If you like soup from smoked bones, you can try it. Keep the meat and bones in the freezer.

Potatoes with Sweet Cream

4 potatoes	= 4
1 qt. water	= 32 ozs.
1 cup farmer's sweet cream (fresh country unpasteurized)	= 250 ml
1 tbsp. salt and ½ tsp. pepper	= 15 ml, 1 ml
1 small onion	= 1

After you have the potatoes boiled, cut them into 1-inch squares or pieces. Also boil small onion heads (young onions) in separate pot till they are almost soft. Next, take the onions, cut them into small pieces and put them into the pot, together with the potatoes. Add salt and pepper, and pour cream to it. Cover the pot with a lid, put it in the oven at 300° F = 150° C and cook the slightly raw potatoes and onions 5 to 10 minutes. If more cream is needed, add more and heat.

Once they were boiling on top of the stove, next they will finish up in the oven. Having them cook in the oven will help to flavorize them together. Do not let the cream dry up. If prepared this way, they are the most delicious potatoes you can eat. Good to eat with fried eggs the same way, or with carrots prepared the same way. Can serve 4. Young potatoes are the best. If young potatoes are boiled, leave them whole. There is no vegetable more starchy then potatoes after they overboil.

• Young potatoes are more delicious than the old. But they don't have the same advantages of "old". They cannot be eaten with most foods, as the old potatoes can. You get more tired of young potatoes. They are also a bit too sweet. The sweetness of young potatoes (flavor) disappears when they mature, like youth in people disappears when they mature.

Carrots with Sweet Cream

4 young carrots	= 4
1 qt. water	= 32 ozs.
1 tbsp. salt and ¼ tsp. pepper	= 15 ml, 1 ml
1 cup cream	= 50 ml

Carrots can be prepared the same way as potatoes. Young garden carrots are the best. Sweet cream cannot be obtained in the city stores, because the dairy products are pasteurized and they are different when treated with heat. Cream cannot be fried like country cream. Sweet cream is fresh cream separated from milk. It hasn't soured nor thickened yet. Unpasteurized products are of olden days. Real delicious, country foods are not known anymore in the city. They are forgotten. And to be able to bring these same dairy products back into the picture, they would have to do the way they did in the olden days. Add cream to the carrots, add salt and pepper, and put it in the oven for 5 to 10 minutes. They are most good with potatoes prepared the same way. Serves 4.

Dried Mushrooms

There are four kinds of wild edible mushrooms in the continent of North America. Clean them and put them to dry out in the sun. If you want to do the job faster, put them on a wide pan, salt them, and place them in the oven, on low heat. After they have dried, store them away, To prepare them, soak in cold water and put them to boil. After they are ready, see that there is a small amount of water left. Chop a small onion and let it boil till the onions are soft. Add salt, pepper and oil. Next, add 1 tablespoon of flour to the juice from mushrooms and make batter. Put it into the pot and let boil for 5 minutes. Good with such food as potatoes. It's served in a small bowl and eaten with a spoon. If prepared in a small pot, it can serve several people.

Canned Meat

2 lbs. beef or pork	= 908 g.
1 whole onion	= 1
2 qts. water	= 64 ozs.
1 tbsp. salt and ½ tsp. hot pepper	= 15ml, 2 ml
1 tsp. black pepper	= 5 ml
6 whole cloves garlic	= 6

Take a large pot and fill ¾ of it with water. Bring to a boil. Add salt, black pepper, and hot pepper. Cut the meat into small pieces and add to the pot. Boil the meat for 2 hours and 15 minutes. After 1 hour add the whole onion. After 2 hours add garlic. Hot pepper can be omitted, if preferred. Allow it to cool and then put into sealers and seal tight. Put them away in a cool, dark place. Let it jell in sealers.

• Too many cooks can spoil the stew, unless they follow the same recipe.

Whole Milk Cottage Cheese

When you have enough whole milk and you want to make homemade cottage cheese, place the pot of milk in a warm room and allow it to get sour till it's thick and lumpy. This is the kind that you can put into a cup and eat it with bread. You don't need to salt it at all. When a bit is added, it will be greatly noticed. It is delicious as well as healthy. Now it is ready to be placed in the pot on a low heated stove and allow it to boil slowly. When you see curds coming together and dividing from the juice, move it from the heat and let it cool. It is now ready to pour into the cheesecloth and allow the rest of the liquid to drip. You can use several bags in succession. Cheesecloths make small bags. This way, it drains better and mixes better with fresh air. It also preserves and keeps it fresh, while trying to use up the package. Cheese also tastes better when it is allowed to stay for several hours. Break the seal and add it to a dish; treat it with country-style sour cream. Delicious to serve, especially with fresh, boiled mashed potatoes. It is gold on your platter! Store the rest in a cool, dark place.

Cheese made from whole milk gives a better flavor, because it contains cream in cheese from whole milk. When it is made from skim milk, the flavor is not as rich. It could be not only delicious, but fattening. Those who worked on a farm had no chance to get fat. A word of caution: great care has to be taken not to boil too long or rapidly or the curds will be overdone, becoming too hard. Or if they are not boiled enough, they will be too soft. So it takes care to prepare them properly. This way, you can get good, rich cottage cheese.

• The country way was different from the city's way. They lived under different conditions; food was different. Instead of buying, they had their own. Preparing food rather than buying, they had fresh products, and preparing most of their home-cooked food made it more economical. Besides, their food tasted better. Consider long ago, they did many things better, like curing bacon, keeping meat and fish and other food in the cold, open air, which helped retain its flavor. Dairy products were fresh and not pasteurized, and chemicals were not used. They put their dairy products to use so that they had good food, even unknown to the cities. Times are changing, and farmers have more money now. They don't prepare food anymore, but they buy ready made-food. And the custom of country food is phasing out. One reason is that they are trying to get away from work. Some of the good customs will vanish forever if they are not reconsidered. And one of the good things in life is country food. And this can be saved by a reminder with recipes.

Helpful Hints

Different ingredients to include in a recipe to make soup or a meal: these are not all put in the pot at the same time. Some ingredients need to boil longer than others. Proper timing with each ingredient will prevent overcooking some of the ingredients that need a short time. Also each ingredient should not be overloaded in the pot. Each ingredient is considered by how much it needs to cook. So the ones that are harder need to be put in first. Then others that are softer need to be put in later. Some ingredients that need a short time to get ready are put in later. So timing with ingredients, you make a proper meal or soup, and they have flavor. If some of the ingredients cook too long, it will not have good flavor. Another way to retain flavor is with the carrots; they can be put to boil whole, and they go in among the first ingredients, like meat, peas, rice, etc. Among the second longest cooking ingredients are potatoes, onions (whole), and some other things. Third, other softer ingredients are put in still later. So these rules are very important to follow!

In other words, if you obey the rules, they will help you do the work properly. The good food is right in front of you only if you obey the rules, and they will do the work for you! Fourth, to retain flavor, it is well to use half the amount of salt and pepper at the beginning, and the other half of it towards the end. This way, salt and pepper will treat the food, and the other half, added to the food, will flavorize the food. So these rules are very important to know and to use them properly. If you obey them, you will be a good cook, and your food will be good also.

• Sweet fresh unpasteurized cream, when fried, will shrink more than any other oil, under heat.

• Depends on ingredients to make soup. To make good soup, it also depends on good water. There is no vegetable more amazing or stubborn than a potato.

If your utensils are stained and cannot be cleaned with detergent, use Jovex fluid. Put all the utensils in a flat metal pan. Add water and the Jovex fluid, and let it soak for a few minutes. Next, take out the utensils and wash them in hot water and detergent. Rinse them in clean water and dry. Your utensils will sparkle. Please note that Jovex is a powerful cleansing fluid, less is used for dishes than for utensils and pots.

FIVE

SANDWICHES AND TOAST

Sandwiches and Toast

Chop green onions fine. Add them to whole milk cottage cheese. Add sour cream and salt; mix well. Good for sandwiches and toast. If it was made of 8 slices of bread, it will make 4 sandwiches. Serves 2.

Chop green onions fine. Add sour cream and salt; mix well. Good for sandwiches. Serves 2.

Egg Sandwiches

Take 2 eggs, beat them. Add salt and pepper. Pour ½ a cup of cereal cream, mix well (or milk will do). Bring it to a boil for a few minutes till it thickens. Stir occasionally, so it doesn't stick to the bottom. Good for take-out sandwiches. Serves 2.

Garlic Toast

After you make some toast, cut up several cloves of garlic into fine pieces. Butter the toast and apply crumbs of garlic over the toast. For the benefit of better tasting toast, do not use too much garlic, as it will make it too bitter, and you won't be able to taste the delicacy of the rest of the toast as you would like to. But you can use as much garlic or as little as you want. Having the garlic chopped fine reduces the bitterness in toast.

Onion Sandwiches

Take as many slices of bread as you need; butter them. Slice a raw onion thin, lay slices on buttered bread, salt it. Good to eat right away, while it is crisp. But if you take them out and wait with them a considerable time, the onions soften. They make delicious sandwiches.

Salted Sandwiches

Take several slices of bread, spread peanut butter over them, then sprinkle a bit of salt. There is nothing new about this. But insofar as that peanut butter is not salted and you would like some salt, you salt the sandwiches. It's for those who like more salt.

SIX

PASTRIES AND BUNS, ETC.

Buns of Bread Dough

Take some bread dough that is prepared for baked bread. Cut it up into small balls. Spread the dough flat. Next, prepare some fillings: cut up some green onions. Add this to cottage cheese and salt it. Add a bit of oil to cheese, so it's not dry, and add some-cut up dill leaves. Do not overuse any of these, but a large amount of filling is good. There are times when you eat them, that you just wish there was more of this filling in these buns. There is no doubt they are the best buns in this cookbook. And since country-style, homemade baking is not done anymore, at times, we may come to think of it and want some, but there is none. That was the way they baked on the farms, because things were available and it was even economical to prepare good food. Now that the filling is ready, take some in a spoon, put it on the flattened dough, and roll it up into a ball. You do this to each bun till you fill the pan. Next, put it in an oven at 300° F = 150° C till they rise and brown. Take them out and let cool. They are very delicious when they are cold. Making dough for a pastry may not do as well, although you would have to use soda or baking powder for dough to rise. This kind of baking is nowhere found in stores, except in the country, and that may be phasing out. It is quite possible baking can be started in the cities and continue as long as they want. Piecrust recipes are available in this cookbook. These can be the queen of all buns! Just that these ingredients can be available in the early months of the summer in the garden.

Homemade Cinnamon Rolls

Take some bread dough and spread it out. Roll it flat and thin with a rolling pin. Take a small sponge like a cloth, and moisten the top of the dough with oil. Next, sprinkle sugar over the dough, and then with cinnamon. Spread it even all over. Now you are ready to roll the dough into a cylinder. After this is done, take a knife and slice the rolls up into 1½ ins. Place the slices one at a time in a wide, flat pan, already greased with oil. (Flour can be used.) Put it in the oven at 300° F = 150°C and let stand till they rise and brown. Remove from the oven and let cool. They are delicious eaten cold!

Pancake Bread Dough

Do you want something different, perhaps a sugar-free pancake? Try this: Take some bread dough, the kind of dough you use to bake bread. After this dough rises, first, cut it into small balls, then spread it out, flattening, making it thin. Then put them in a hot, greasy frying pan. Let them brown on one side. Then turn them over to fry the other side, adding some oil each time they are turned. See that the dough is thin and fries well. They taste better when they are still fresh and warm. Good for a snack! Of course it is not good to eat them often. But once in a while, it is all right. They are unlike the cinnamon rolls, which are best eaten cold. But pancake bread dough is best eaten hot, even though it is made of the same dough.

Cheddar Cheese Buns

Take some bread dough and cut it into small balls. Spread it out flat. Now fill it with cheddar cheese, then roll them up into balls, and place them in a wide, flat pan. You can use a bit of flour for the pan, instead of oil. Put them in the oven at 325°F = 160°C till they brown. Delicious to eat them after they cool.

Buns with Cinnamon Apple

Take some bread dough and cut it into small balls. Spread the dough flat. Now fill it with cheddar cheese. Roll them up into apple shapes, treated with sugar and cinnamon. Roll them up into small buns, place them in a wide, flat oiled pan, and put them in an oven at 300°F = 150°C till they brown. After they are ready, take them out and cool.

Onion Buns

Take some bread dough and cut it into small balls. Spread the dough out flat. Now fill it with chopped green onions, a bit of salt with oil added to it. Now roll them up into small buns, put them in a wide, flat oiled pan, and put them in the oven at 300°F = 150°C till they brown. Then take them out and let cool. My! What a treat.

Carrot Buns

Take some of the bread dough and cut it into small balls. Spread them out flat, and fill them with boiled, mashed carrots. Have them salted and oiled. When you have put the filling over, close it up and roll them into balls. Put them in a wide, flat oiled pan and place it in the oven at 300°F = 150°C till they brown and are ready. Remove from the oven and let cool.

Banana Buns

Take some bread dough and cut it into small balls. Spread them flat. Now have banana filling prepared: mash some bananas, add sugar and cinnamon, and a bit of oil. Mix. Spread the filling over them and roll them into balls. Put them in a wide oiled (flour can be used) pan and put them in the oven at 300°F = 150°C till brown. Remove them from the heat and let cool.

Potato Buns

Take some bread dough and cut it into small balls. Spread them flat. Next, have some boiled, mashed potatoes ready. Add salt and pepper and a bit of oil and mix it. Spread this filling on the dough and roll them into balls. Put them in a wide oiled pan and in the oven at 300° F = 150° C till they brown and are ready. Remove from heat and let cool. For potato buns, the potatoes don't need to be soft, since they go into the oven again. But they have to be mashed and well-oiled, etc.

Piecrust

1 lb. flour	= 454 g.
¼ cup oil	= 60 ml
½ tsp. salt	= 2 ml
½ cup milk or water	= 125 ml
1 tsp. sugar	= 5 ml
1 tsp. baking powder	= 5 ml

Put the flour into a mixing bowl. Add baking powder, salt, sugar and oil, and mix it well. Then knead it with clean hands to mix well. Pour milk or water and stir with a spoon till you get the dough in a right consistency. If dough is sticky, add a bit of flour and mix till the dough gets to be the kind that can be handled without it sticking. Cut and flatten small pieces in 2" to 3" size, and put them in the oven in an oiled pan at 300° F = 150° C till it browns. These can be made for eating as well as for piecrust.

Potato Patties

2 potatoes	= 2
1 small onion	= 1
2 tbsps. flour	= 25 ml
½ tsp. salt and ¼ tsp. pepper	= 2 ml, 1 ml
Oil for frying	

Take boiled, cold potatoes and mash them. Add salt and black pepper, chopped onion, and flour and mix. See that it doesn't stick together, when trying to make them into balls. More flour will prevent this. Make them into small balls and flatten them, then put them one by one in a frying pan. Be sure to have enough oil and that the pan is hot. You might find that the onions don't stay together. It is better to chop onions into tiny pieces so they won't be sticking out. Have both sides fried well, adding oil each time you turn them over. By not using enough oil, they may go dry. Do not use too much oil. Use a flat spoon to turn them over. If you make small patties, they will taste better. Now you can have a very delicious meal! Serves 2 (Eat them hot.)

Buttermilk Biscuits

3 cups flour	= 750 ml
4 tsps. baking powder	= 20 ml
1 tsp. salt	= 5 ml
4 tbsps. butter	= 60 ml
½ cup sugar	= 125 ml
2 eggs	= 2
2 cups buttermilk	= 250 ml

Put flour into a mixing bowl. Add baking powder, salt, sugar, and melt butter. Mix well. Pour in buttermilk and beaten eggs, then stir till you get the right dough (soft). If the dough is too soft or thick, add more flour or liquid. Have additional flour to form the biscuits into balls. Put them in a wide oiled (flour will do as substitute for oil) pan, then put them in an oven at 300° F = 150° C. Let stay till they rise and brown. Delicious with tea and coffee. Should yield at least 2 dozen. Serves 10 to 12.

Buttermilk Pancakes

1 cup flour	= 8 ozs.
2 tsps. soda	= 10 ml
¼ tsp. salt	= 1 ml
2 tsps. sugar	= 10 ml
1 tsp. vanilla	= 5 ml
1 cup buttermilk	= 8 ozs.

Add flour to a mixing bowl. Add soda, salt, and sugar and mix it well. No oil for pancakes. They get enough oil used for the pan. They are the greasiest pastries of all. Now pour in buttermilk and beaten eggs to make the batter of right thickness, then use a fork to mix. Have vanilla added to buttermilk. Use a large spoon to put dough into a frying pan, two or three spoons to make small pancakes. You can decide what size pancakes you want. Small pancakes, fried in sufficient oil, taste better, than larger ones in insufficient oil. Have both sides fried well, adding oil each time you put others in and turning them over. You can use syrup or eat them without. As for myself, I like them without syrup. If you have them stay overnight or for next meal, they will get cold in the fridge and become even more delicious eaten cold. They taste wonderful with hot coffee for breakfast. Serves 2.

Cheese Pancakes

First, take a small pot of water. Add ½ teaspoon poppy seeds, 1 teaspoon of bran, and a bit of salt. Let it boil for 5 minutes. Then remove from heat and let it cool. Pour milk or cereal cream in, then you can have pancake flour put in and stir with a fork till it gets the right batter for pancakes. Next, take 1 tablespoon of cheddar cheese and mix it with a bit of water, using a fork for mixing. Then put the batter in a mixing bowl, and stir well. Now the dough is ready to put in an oily frying pan, making the pancakes about 3 inches in diameter. Some pancakes with enough oil have better taste than big ones with a bit of oil. Serves 2.

- The dough absorbs the onion and garlic flavors more than any ingredients.
- The heat will get through thin dough easier than through thick dough and cook the inside.

Carrot Pancakes

1 carrot	=	1
½ cup pancake powder	=	125 ml
A bit salt		
½ cup milk or water	=	125 ml

Pour milk or water into a small pot. Add salt, pancake powder and mashed carrot (already boiled carrot). Mix it well with a fork till you get the batter just right. Now have a hot oily frying pan ready. Take a large spoon and spoon out 2 or 3 times to make a pancake. Let them fry till you see holes puncturing the top of pancakes and they are drying up. This lets you know that they are soon to be ready on the bottom and need to be turned over. Oil the pan each time you put in the dough. Remember, they are like fried potatoes. If you don't add enough oil, they won't be good. When making dough, if you think you have added enough flour and it looks thick, just take a fork and beat the dough. This will thin it. Don't pour a bit of water in it instead. This may make it thin again. Delicious to eat them hot or warm. Serves 2.

Onion and Garlic Pancakes

1 tbsp. chopped onion	=	15 ml
1 tbsp. chopped garlic	=	15 ml
½ tsp. poppy seed	=	2 ml
½ tbsp. bran	=	8 ml
½ cup water	=	125 ml
½ cup milk	=	125 ml
Salt		
½ cup pancake powder	=	125 ml

Pour ½ cup of water into a small pot, add a bit of salt, bran, poppy seed, onion and garlic. Allow it to boil for 5 minutes. Remove from the stove and let cool so it won't be too hot for milk to be poured in. After you have the milk in, add the pancake powder and mix it with a fork till you get the right pancake dough. Have the large spoon ready and dip out a few spoons of dough to make a pancake on a hot, oily frying pan. Do not raise the heat high, keep it about 23 minutes past the hour. When you see holes on top of the pancakes, they are about ready to be turned over: use oil each time. Serves 2.

SEVEN

SALADS

Potato Salad

4 potatoes	= 4
2 eggs	= 2
1 bunch green onions	= 1
6 radishes	= 6
6 leaves lettuce	= 6
½ tsp. salt	= 2 ml
2 tbsps. vinegar	= 25 ml

Make a salad consisting of the following proportions: 3/4 of potatoes and 2 eggs to only ¼ of vegetables. For best results, prepare the vegetables, cut them up, salt them and sprinkle vinegar over them. Mix them well. Let the vegetables stand in vinegar and salt for several hours. Next, slice the cold, boiled potatoes and the 2 hard-boiled eggs. Add together and salt it, and mix it with a spoon. Add sour cream as much as you need. Mix with a large spoon. Since there is a large amount of salad prepared, it is best to salt and add vinegar and sour cream, some at a time, and this is the way you can have it prepared better. Ready to serve a large family.

Potato, Vegetable Salad

1 potato	=	1
1 egg	=	1
12 leaves lettuce	=	12
6 radishes	=	6
1 bunch green onions	=	1
½ tsp. salt	=	2 ml
2 tbsps. vinegar	=	25 ml
Sour cream	=	250 ml
1 ripe tomato	=	1

Cut up the vegetables and put them into large bowl, salt and sprinkle vinegar evenly over them. Mix well with a large spoon. Next, slice the cold, boiled potato and the hard-boiled egg and put them into the bowl. Salt and sprinkle vinegar over. Mix well. Add sour cream and mix it again. Enough to serve a large family.

Raw Salad (Cole Slaw)

2 carrots	=	2
1 celery stalk	=	1
¼ tsp. salt	=	2 ml
1 tsp. oil	=	5 ml
1 tbsp. vinegar	=	15 ml

Scrape the skin of the carrots, then grind them and the celery in a blender. Add salt, oil, and vinegar to them. Mix them well. For best results, let them stay first in vinegar, etc. Put them in small jars, to keep its freshness when being used. Store it away in a cool, dark place. It's best served when it is cold, with a meal. Do not grind raw salad too thin.

Saskatoon Leaf Salad

After you have made a salad, decorate it on top with some young, clean Saskatoon leaves. By the way, Saskatoon leaves are good to eat at the time when they are young and tender, around blossom time.

Rose Petal Salad

Make a potato vegetable salad—or any salad will do. Put some clean, fresh rose petals that you may pick from the roses. Now set them on top to decorate the salad. Oh, what a dainty dish to set before the king!

Raw Cabbage and Tomato Salad

Slice and cut the cabbage and ripe tomatoes. Add salt and vinegar to it, mix well. Sour cream can be added to it. Good served with a meal.

Green and Red Pepper Salad

Slice the sweet peppers. You can slice raw cabbage and ripe tomatoes and lettuce. Add salt and sprinkle some vinegar on it; mix it. Put it in sealers and place them in cool, dark place. Good with a meal.

• Vinegar is a flavorizer as a preserver of food.

EIGHT

DESSERTS

Raisin Rhubarb Pie

2 cups rhubarb	= 500 ml
½ cup raisins	= 125 ml
1 tbsp. lemon juice	= 15 ml
½ cup white sugar	= 125 ml
Salt, oil and water	
1 cup flour	= 250 ml
1 tsp. cornstarch	= 15 ml

First, make crusts for the pie, one for the bottom of the pie plate, and one for the top of the pie. Before putting the filling on the bottom crust, first put the dough on the pie plate and put in the oven till it browns, because if you are going to put raw rhubarb on the unbrowned crust, it will soak the dough when the rhubarb starts releasing its juice, so the crust is not going to cook and brown for the pie as it should. The filler is just going to soak and make it doughy. So if the crust is being put in the oven first, this is not going to happen.

To prepare the filling is as follows: Let the raisins soak for a while, so as to soften them. Next, cut the rhubarb up into ½-inch pieces. Put all the rhubarb onto the crust, then put the raisins in. Add sugar, oil, and lemon juice. For the rest of the portion, make batter, add cornstarch to 2 tablespoons of flour, add a few tablespoons of lemon juice and make batter with a fork. Then put this batter in together with the rest in the pie. There is no need of liquid, as there will be enough juice.

To make a pie crust: put flour into a mixing bowl, add salt, oil, and water. First add salt and oil to the flour, then mix and knead on the flour. After this is done, pour water into it, and make dough of it. After you have made the proper dough free from sticking to your hands, roll the dough out flat with a rolling pin. If the dough is still sticky, add some flour and finish up. You have one layer of the crust on the pie plate. The other layer that is to go on top; first set on the board and fold it in two, then cut holes, cutting right through both layers. When you put this layer on top of the pie, it will allow the steam to come out through these holes. After you are finished with the pie, put it in the oven at 300° F = 150° C till it browns. Then remove it out of the oven and allow it to cool.

Should serve about 5 or 6. A pie with these with these ingredients should be kept 10 to 15 minutes longer than some other pies.

Wild Cranberry Pie

2½ cups cranberries	= 625 ml
½ cup sugar	= 125 ml
Oil	
½ tsp. salt	= 2 ml
1 tbsp. cornstarch	= 15 ml
2 cups flour	= 2 cups
Water (Use warm water only)	= 2 cups

First prepare the dough for a crust. Take the flour and mix it in a container with salt and oil. Mix it and knead the dough: that will do for a crust. Add water and mix well. If the dough sticks to your hands, add some flour and knead it till it is right for a crust. Take 1 layer of dough and fold it in two. Cut holes through both layers, in the one that will go on top. These holes are for the steam to come out, preventing too much water in the pie. The cranberries don't have as much juice as the rhubarb has, and the bottom crust may not have to go in the oven twice. Rhubarb is the pie filler that has the most juice. Now prepare the filling: wash the berries and leave the pecks in. put raw berries into a container, add sugar. *To make batter:* add 2 tablespoons flour, 1 teaspoon of cornstarch, add 2 tablespoons of water. Take a fork and make batter. Then add all to the filling for the pie; cover the top of the pie with the other layer of dough. Next press the dough all around the edge, so it will stick to the pie plate. Now you can put it in the oven at 300° F = 150° C till it's ready and brown. Then take it out, and let it cool. Serves 5 or 6. A very delicious cranberry pie!

The Gingerbread Dolly

2 cups flour	= 500 ml
2 eggs	= 2
2 tsps. baking powder	= 10 ml
¼ tsp. salt	= 1 ml
½ tsp. vanilla	= 2 ml
2 tsps. ginger	= 10 ml
1 cup milk	= 250 ml
¼ cup sugar	= 60 ml

Mix the dry ingredients: flour, baking powder, ginger and salt together. Add liquid ingredients in the other container, and stir well. If too thin, add more flour and stir till you get a medium consistency in the dough for a cake. Next pour into a 8"x 8" size pan. Put it in the oven at 350 ° F = 180° C for ten minutes. Then bake at 300° F = 150° C till it rises and browns. Next, take it out the oven and let it cool. Serves 8 to 10.

Chocolate Cake

2 cups flour	= 500 ml
1 egg	= 1
1/3 cup sugar	= 80 ml
¼ tsp. salt	= 1 ml
½ tsp. vanilla	= 2 ml
4 tbsps. cocoa	= 60 ml
2 tbsps. melted butter	= 30 ml
1½ cup milk	= 375 ml
2 tbsps. crushed walnuts	= 60 ml

Use 1 mixing bowl to make batter for a cake. Beat the egg and pour warm milk in; add salt, vanilla, melted butter, sugar and crushed walnuts. Mix it well with a fork. In the other mixing bowl, add flour, cocoa, baking powder, and salt. Mix it well with a fork. Now put the flour, etc., into the batter, and stir it up well. If the batter is too thin, add a bit of flour, and if too thick, add a bit of milk, stir again. Test the cake batter to see if it has enough salt. Now pour this batter into 8"x 8" pan. To prepare the bottom pan first, you can use a bit of flour instead of oil so the cake doesn't stick to the pan. Waxed paper can be used as well. Put the cake in the oven at 350° F = 180° C for 10 minutes at first, then turn it down to 300° F = 150° C and let it bake till it rises and browns. It is a good idea to take a stem of a broom and poke it into the cake. If the stem is moist and has crumbs, it needs to stay a bit longer. If it's dry, the cake is ready baked. Take it out of the oven and let cool. You can apply chocolate icing on top, thick or thin. To make the icing, add a few tablespoons of cocoa to 1 teaspoon of sugar and a few spoons of milk or water. Put it back in the oven for a few minutes. Let it cool. Serves 8 to 10.

NINE

FRUITS

Saskatoon-Rhubarb Fruit

2 qts. Saskatoon berries	= 8 cups—64 ozs.
1 qt. rhubarb	= 32 ozs.
½ qt. sugar	= 16 ozs.
2 qts. water	= 64 ozs.
A few tbsps. lemon juice	= 25 ml

Put berries and the cut-up rhubarb into a big pot of 2 quarts of water. Add sugar and lemon juice to the fruit. Let it soak for several hours. Put to boil. When it starts to boil, watch for the foam rising, then lower the heat immediately and see that it continues to boil slow. Do not boil this fruit rapidly, but rather let it boil under low heat. It doesn't take long for fruit to soften. Rhubarb is the kind that needs more sugar, so taste to see if it needs more. When it is done remove it from heat, then pour into sealers and seal tight. Store them away in cool, a dark place.

Raisin Rhubarb

2 qts. rhubarb	= 64 ozs.
½ cup raisins	= 125 ml
2 cups sugar	= 16 ozs.
1 qt. water	= 32 ozs.
2 tbsps. lemon juice	= 25 ml
2 tbsps. lemon and orange peelings	= 25 ml

Cut the rhubarb into 1-inch pieces, and put it in a pot together with the raisins, sugar, lemon juice, and fruit peelings and water. Let it soak for several hours. See that you don't have too much water. Boil at low heat till it gets soft. Let it cool, then pour into sealers, seal tight, and put them away in a cool, dark place.

• Humans eat the least fresh food of any other fleshly creatures.

Pincherry Jam

2 qts. pincherries	= 64 ozs.
2 cups sugar	= 500 ml
1 qt. water	= 32 ozs.

First, clean and wash the berries. Put them in together with sugar and water. Boil them at 300° F = 150° C till you notice they get soft. Pardon me, let the berries boil in water, without sugar first. Then remove them from the heat, and pour them into a mesh, and squeeze the berries with a wooden tool, to squeeze the juice out of them, separating the pecks from them. Next, have the juice boil till it gets thick. Taste to see if it needs more sugar; add some to help it to thicken into jam. Care must be taken not to have too much water or boil too long. When this satisfies the cook, pour into small jars and seal tight. Store them away in a cool, dark place. One of the best jams you will find.

Black Currant Jam

2 qts. currant berries	= 64 ozs.
2 cups sugar	= 500 ml
1 qt. water	= 32 ozs.

First clean and wash the berries and put them into a pot of water. Put them to boil at medium heat at first for 5 minutes, then lower the heat to low. Boil them till they get soft. Now they are ready to be squeezed, separating the juice and skin from the pecks. Put the juice to boil again along with the sugar till it thickens into jam. Pour into small jars and seal tight. Store them away in a cool, dark place.

• Pincherries are the only fruit that grows on the tallest shrubberries. They also are the only fruit that ripens all at one time, unlike the other fruits, in which some ripen while others are still green. It has a sharp taste and its color is red, with a tinge of purple. The taste of fruit made from them is not so good. But they make the most delicious jams and jellies. Pincherries have two qualities, usual and unusual: usual qualities of jams and jellies, unusual taste of fruit made from them. They don't grow in abundance in Manitoba, Canada.

Strawberry Dessert

Fill a cup with 3/4 cup of wild strawberries, ¼ cup of farmer's sweet cream or cereal cream, and 1 teaspoon of sugar. Crush the berries with a spoon and stir it up. You can eat it with bread or without. Very delicious to the taste. Prepared in 1 cup, will serve 1 person.

Raspberry Dessert

Fill the cup with 3/4 of raspberries, ¼ cup of farmer's sweet cream or cereal cream, and 1 teaspoon of sugar. Crush the berries with the spoon and stir it up. You can eat it with or without bread. Or you can put some on your toast. Delicious! Serves 1.

Blueberry Dessert

Want to try something different? Take 6 cups of berries and put them into a large bowl. Add 6 teaspoons of sugar and 1 cup of sweet cream. Beat 1 egg well with an egg beater. Add ½ teaspoon of vanilla, stir well. Delicious! Serves 6.

Banana Canteloupe Dessert

Slice up 3 bananas and 1/3 of a canteloupe into small pieces. Add a few teaspoons of sugar and ½ cup of sweet cream or cereal cream, stir well. Should serve 5 to 6.

• Wild berries and cherries have stronger flavor, are like wildflowers, have stronger scent.

• If you had wildflowers instead of domestic flowers in your flower shop, the scent in the shop would be so strong that it could possibly be noticed 1 or 2 blocks away.

TEN
BEVERAGES

Lemon-Tea Drink

Take 1 lemon and cut it in two. Squeeze the juice out. Pour it into a cup, add sugar. In a teapot, brew tea from the leaves for 5 minutes. After this, drain it through a cheesecloth into the pot where lemon juice is, stir well. It can make as much as 3 cups of beverage. You can use honey as well as sugar. Good to drink hot or cold. Serves 3.

Wine-Tea Drink

Pour hot boiling water to a teapot with 2 or 3 teaspoons of tea leaves and let it brew for 5 minutes. Separate tea from leaves through cheesecloth. Add sugar and wine to the tea. Good to drink it hot or cold. Enjoyable when guests are invited. Serves 3. A larger amount can be prepared, if needed.

Hot Pepper in Tea or Coffee

Put a small piece of hot pepper into the teapot, with tea leaves or coffee in it. Let it brew for 5 minutes in hot boiling water. Serve it into cups, add sugar and cream. Can be made to serve several people.

Grapefruit-Tea Drink

Cut the fruit in two, squeeze the juice out. Pour ready-tea into the grape juice. Add sugar and stir. If a larger amount is needed, add more juice to the drink. Two grapefruits may serve 4.

Prune-Tea Drink

Have the prunes boil in a pot with a little water. Do not have much water, because you need the juice to be stronger for a drink with tea. For better results, it is good to add 1/3 to 2/3 of a cup of tea. Add sugar and cream and stir; 2 cups of juice will serve 6.

• Every time you drink a cup of coffee, you always stick your nose in. Long noses get in deeper, whether they have any business to be or not.

• Most foods you cannot eat without salt. But you don't need any salt for fruit.

Orange-Tea Drink

Take 1 orange and cut it in two. Squeeze the juice into a glass, add sugar. Brew tea in a teapot for 5 minutes. Next, drain it through a cheesecloth and pour it into a glass with the juice and sugar and stir. Good to drink hot or cold. Serves 1.

Raisin-Juice Drink

Boil raisins with sugar for 10 to 15 minutes. See that you use only a little water. Pour the juice into a glass to 1/3 level. Brew tea for 5 minutes, then drain it and pour into the glass where the juice is. Delicious drink! Serves 1.

Cocoa Drink

Add 1 teaspoon of cocoa and 1 or 2 teaspoons of sugar to a cup. First, pour a bit of hot water in the cup, stir the batter, then pour a full cup of boiling water, and stir. Add cream to the cocoa. Delicious to drink it hot. Serves 1. Or you can boil milk and add cocoa and sugar to the drink. Farm milk is the best to boil. (Just bring it up to a boil.)

Lemon-Milk Drink

Bring farmer's milk to a boil; add 1 teaspoon of sugar. Pour it into about ¼ cup of lemon juice. Delicious to drink it hot. Serves 1.

Chokecherry-Tea Drink

Boil the cherries for about 15 minutes with a little water so the juice will be strong. Separate the pecks from the juice; add sugar. On the other hand, brew tea for 5 minutes. Then pour into the cup 1/3 filled with juice. Tea is only good to drink while it still is fresh. Delicious to drink it hot. One glass of juice will make 3 cups.

Cranberry-Tea Drink

Boil cranberries with sugar and a bit of water for 15 minutes. Remove from the heat and squash the berries to squeeze the juice from them. Add 1/3 of a cup to brewed tea. A delicious drink! Drink it hot and still fresh; 1 glass of juice can serve 3 cups.

Cinnamon-Tea Drink

Cut an apple up and boil it together with sugar and 2 tablespoons of apple cinnamon. Use about 1/3 of a cup to 2/3 of brewed tea. Drink it with or without cream. One glass of juice can make 3 cups. Drink it fresh.

Cold Remedy

1 tablespoon of honey	= 15 ml
1/8-size piece of hot pepper	= 0.5 ml
1 cup water	= 250 ml
½ tsp. tea leaves	= 2 ml

Bring the water to a boil, then pour hot water into the teapot with tea leaves and hot pepper. Allow it to brew for 5 minutes. Then separate tea leaves from the tea. Add 1 tablespoon of honey and stir. Drink it hot! To make twice as much, add twice as much ingredients.

Other drinks, but strong and sour and hot! Use only half of a glass of the juice drink of sauerkraut and dill pickle juice, as these juices are strong and make you thirsty.

• Rhubarb, pumpkins, and citrons are plants or vegetables, but when they are prepared, they become fruits. Citrons are properly called citron fruits (citron melon).

• Cows produce rich dairy products; these are: milk, whole or skim; cream, butter, buttermilk, cottage and cheddar cheese and sour milk. But there is only one that goes to waste: the juice that is separated from the cottage cheese. It is fed to pigs.

• Beets are the hardest of the vegetables, and it takes the longest to boil them.

• Cream is the queen of the plate, and honey is the king of the platter.